No Child Left Behind: Issues and Developments

Paul H. Berkhart
Editor

Nova Science Publishers, Inc.
New York

For permission to use material from this book please contact us:
Telephone 631-231-7269; Fax 631-231-8175
Web Site: http://www.novapublishers.com

LIBRARY OF CONGRESS CATALOGING-IN-PUBLICATION DATA
No Child Left Behind : issues and developments / Paul H. Berkhart, editor.
p. cm.
ISBN 978-1-60456-210-1 (hardcover)
1. Educational accountability--Law and legislation--United States. 2. Federal aid to education--United States. 3. United States. No Child Left Behind Act of 2001. I. Berkhart, Paul H.
KF4195.N6 2007
379.1'580973--dc22

2007047443

Published by Nova Science Publishers, Inc. ✢ New York

CONTENTS

NO CHILD LEFT BEHIND: ISSUES AND DEVELOPMENTS

PREFACE

This new book presents the latest developments related to the the No Child Left Behind Act of 2001, legislation to extend and revise the Elementary and Secondary Education Act (ESEA), which was signed into law as P.L. 107-110 (H.R. 1). This legislation extensively amends and re-authorizes many of the programs of federal aid to elementary and secondary education. Major features of the No Child Left Behind Act of 2001 include the following: (a) states will be required to implement standards-based assessments in reading and mathematics for pupils in each of grades 3-8 by the 2005-2006 school year, and at three grade levels in science by the 2007-2008 school year; (b) grants to states for assessment development are authorized; (c) all states will be required to participate in National Assessment of Educational Progress tests in 4th and 8th grade reading and mathematics every second year; (d) states must develop adequate yearly progress (AYP) standards, incorporating a goal of all pupils reaching a proficient or advanced level of achievement within 12 years, and apply them to each public school, local education agency (LEA), and the state overall; (e) a sequence of consequences, including public school choice and supplemental services options, would apply to schools and LEAs that fail to meet AYP standards for 2 or more consecutive years; (f) ESEA Title I allocation formulas are modified to increase targeting on high poverty states and LEAs and to move Puerto Rico gradually toward parity with the states; (g) within 3 years, all paraprofessionals paid with Title I funds must have completed at least 2 years of higher education or met a "rigorous standard of quality"; (h) several new programs aimed at improving reading instruction are authorized; (i) teacher programs are consolidated into a state grant authorizing a wide range of activities such as teacher recruitment, professional development, and hiring; (j) states and LEAs participating in Title I have various requirements to ensure that teachers meet the bill's definition of "highly qualified" by the end of the 2005-2006 school year; (k) almost all states and LEAs are authorized to transfer a portion of the funds they receive under several programs, and selected states and LEAs may consolidate funds under certain programs through performance agreements; (l) federal support of public school choice is expanded; (m) several previous programs are consolidated into a state grant supporting integration of technology into K-12 education; (n) the Bilingual and Emergency Immigrant Education Acts are consolidated into a single formula grant, with existing limits on the share of grants for specific instructional approaches eliminated; and (o) the 21st Century Community Learning Center program is converted into a formula grant with increased focus on after-school activities.

Chapter 1 - Title I, Part A of the Elementary and Secondary Education Act (ESEA), authorizes financial aid to local educational agencies (LEAs) for the education of disadvantaged children and youth at the preschool, elementary, and secondary levels. Over the last several years, the accountability provisions of this program have been increasingly focused on achievement and other outcomes for participating pupils and schools. Since 1994, and particularly under the No Child Left Behind Act of 2001 (NCLB), a key concept embodied in these requirements is that of "adequate yearly progress (AYP)" for schools, LEAs, and states. AYP is defined primarily on the basis of aggregate scores of various groups of pupils on state assessments of academic achievement. The primary purpose of AYP requirements is to serve as the basis for identifying schools and LEAs where performance is unsatisfactory, so that inadequacies may be addressed first through provision of increased support and, ultimately, a variety of "corrective actions."

Under NCLB, the Title I-A requirements for state-developed standards of AYP were substantially expanded in scope and specificity. Under NCLB, AYP calculations must be disaggregated — that is, determined separately and specifically for not only all pupils but also for several demographic groups of pupils within each school, LEA, and state. In addition, while AYP standards had to be applied previously only to pupils, schools, and LEAs participating in Title I-A, AYP standards under NCLB must be applied to *all* public schools, LEAs, and to states overall, if a state chooses to receive Title I-A grants. However, corrective actions for failing to meet AYP standards need be applied only to schools and LEAs participating in Title I-A. Another major break with the past is that state AYP standards must now incorporate concrete movement toward meeting an ultimate goal of all pupils reaching a proficient or advanced level of achievement by 2014.

The overall percentage of public schools identified as failing to make AYP for one or more years based on test scores in 2004-2005 was approximately 26% of *all* public schools. The percentage of schools for individual states varied from 2% to 66%. Approximately 14% of Title I-A participating schools were in the "needs improvement" status (i.e., they had failed to meet AYP standards for two or more consecutive years) based on AYP determinations for 2004-2005 and preceding school years.

The AYP provisions of NCLB are challenging and complex, and they have generated substantial interest and debate. Debates regarding NCLB provisions on AYP have focused on the provision for an ultimate goal, use of confidence intervals and data-averaging, population diversity effects, minimum pupil group size (n), separate focus on specific pupil groups, number of schools identified and state variations therein, the 95% participation rule, state variations in assessments and proficiency standards, and timing. ESEA programs are authorized through FY2008, and it is generally assumed that the 110th Congress will actively consider legislation to amend and extend the ESEA.

Chapter 2 - A key concept embodied in the accountability provisions of the Elementary and Secondary Education Act (ESEA), as amended by the No Child Left Behind Act of 2001 (NCLB, P.L. 107-110), is that of adequate yearly progress (AYP). In order to be eligible for grants under ESEA Title I, Part A — Education for Disadvantaged Pupils — states must implement AYP policies applicable to all public schools and local educational agencies (LEAs), based primarily on the scores of pupils on state assessments. Schools or LEAs that fail to meet AYP standards for two or more consecutive years face a variety of consequences.

The primary model of AYP under the NCLB is a group status model. Such models set threshold levels of performance, expressed as a percentage of pupils scoring at a proficient or higher level on state assessments of reading and mathematics, that must be met by all pupils as a group, as well as pupils in designated demographic subgroups, in order for a public school or LEA to make AYP. Current law also includes a secondary model of AYP, a "safe harbor" provision, under which a school or LEA may make AYP if, among pupil groups who did not meet the primary AYP standard, the percentage of pupils who are *not* at the proficient or higher level declines by at least 10%.

Substantial interest has been expressed in the possible use of individual/cohort growth models to meet the AYP requirements of the NCLB. Such AYP models are not consistent with certain statutory provisions of the NCLB, as those have until recently been interpreted by the U.S. Department of Education (ED). However, under a pilot program, ED has approved applications from nine states to use growth models to make AYP determinations. Many proponents of growth models of AYP see them as being more fair and accurate than the models generally employed to meet NCLB requirements, primarily because they recognize the fact that different schools and pupils have different starting points in their achievement levels, and recognize progress being made at all levels.

Growth models of AYP have the disadvantage of implicitly setting lower initial thresholds or expectations for some pupil groups and/or schools. Although any growth model consistent with the NCLB would need to incorporate the act's ultimate goal of all pupils at a proficient or higher level of achievement by 2013-2014, such models used currently in state (non-NCLB) accountability plans do not include such goals and might allow disadvantaged schools and pupils to remain at relatively low levels of achievement for significant periods of time. Growth models of AYP may be quite complicated and may address the accountability purposes of the NCLB less directly and clearly than the currently statutory AYP models.

ESEA programs are authorized through FY2008, and it is generally assumed that the 110th Congress will actively consider legislation to amend and extend the ESEA.

Chapter 3 - Educational assistance programs have been authorized for veterans of the Armed Forces since 1944. The Servicemen's Readjustment Act of 1944 (P.L. 78346), or the GI Bill of Rights, provided support, including education benefits, to veterans of World War II. Subsequently, other programs were implemented for similar purposes (e.g., the Korean GI Bill and the Vietnam Era GI Bill). These new programs were primarily, if not exclusively, funded by the federal government and were intended to support veterans returning from war. The implementation of the Post-Vietnam Era Veterans' Educational Assistance Program (VEAP) marked the first time that an educational benefit had been established for an all-volunteer force, serving during a period of peace; the first time that education benefits were viewed as a recruiting tool for the military; and the first time that program participants were required to contribute to the education benefit fund while in the military. Many of the principles of VEAP were carried over during the creation of the Montgomery GI Bill (MGIB), the current military education benefit that was implemented in 1985.

Military education benefits have evolved significantly over the last 60-plus years. For example, military education benefits initially were completely subsidized by the federal government; they were issued to institutions of higher education (IHEs) on behalf of the veteran; and the benefits included subsistence payments and could be used for numerous training and educational programs. Conversely, the current benefits are partially subsidized, paid directly to the student as a subsistence payment, and are limited to specific training and education programs. College prices have substantially changed during this period. For example, in a recent 20-year period (academic years 1985-1986 to 2005-2006), the average tuition, fees, room, and board at a four-year public institution increased by 214% (current dollars). Moreover, the manner in which federal student financial aid is calculated and awarded has shifted several times during the evolution of the military education benefits program. At present, federal student assistance is calculated according to the federal need analysis system, which considers the receipt of military education benefits when determining eligibility for some student aid programs. These policy and program changes have altered the role that military benefits play in providing access to postsecondary education for veterans.

This report provides information about the various military education benefits provided to members of the Armed Forces and how these benefits have changed over time. More specifically, it includes a historical overview of education benefits for military veterans, an analysis of the estimated value of these benefits with respect to the average college price, and a discussion of the interaction between military education benefits and federal student aid benefits authorized by Title IV of the Higher Education Act of 1965 (HEA), as amended.

Chapter 4 - The primary source of federal aid to K-12 education is the Elementary and Secondary Education Act (ESEA), particularly its Title I, Part A program of Education for the Disadvantaged. The ESEA was initially enacted in 1965 (P.L. 89-10), and was most recently amended and reauthorized by the No Child Left Behind Act of 2001 (NCLBA, P.L. 107-110). Virtually all ESEA programs are authorized through FY2008. During the current 110th Congress, congressional hearings are being conducted in anticipation of subsequent consideration of legislation to amend and extend the ESEA.

The NCLBA initiated a major expansion of federal influence upon several aspects of public K-12 education, primarily with the aim of increasing the accountability of public school systems and individual public schools for improving achievement outcomes of all pupils, especially the disadvantaged. States must implement in all public schools and school districts a variety of standards-based assessments in reading, math and science; make complex annual adequate yearly progress (AYP) determinations for each public school and district; and require virtually all public school teachers and aides to meet a variety of qualification requirements. State AYP policies must incorporate an ultimate goal of all public school pupils reaching a proficient or higher level of achievement by the end of the 2013-14 school year. Further, participating states must enforce a series of increasingly substantial consequences for most of their schools and almost all school districts that fail to meet the AYP standards for two consecutive years or more. All of these requirements are associated with state participation in the ESEA Title I-A program.

Other major ESEA programs provide grants to support the education of migrant students; recruitment of and professional development for teachers; language instruction for limited English proficient students; drug abuse prevention programs; after-school instruction and care; expansion of charter schools and other forms of public school choice; education services for Native American, Native Hawaiian, and Alaska Native students; Impact Aid to compensate local educational agencies for taxes foregone due to certain federal activities; and a wide variety of innovative educational approaches or instruction to meet particular student needs.

This report provides a brief overview of major provisions of the ESEA. It will not be updated.

Chapter 5 - One of the major goals of the No Child Left Behind Act of 2001 (NCLB) is to raise the achievement of students who currently fail to meet grade-level proficiency standards. Since student achievement is believed by many to depend in large part on effective teaching, the law also contains provisions designed to improve teacher quality. These provisions establish minimum teacher quality requirements and charge states and school districts with developing plans to meet them. These plans are to ensure that all schools have a *highly qualified teacher* in every classroom by the end of the 2005-2006 school year.

To be deemed *highly qualified*, NCLB requires that teachers possess a baccalaureate degree and a state teaching certificate, and that teachers also demonstrate subject-matter knowledge for their teaching level. Elementary school teachers must show knowledge of basic elementary school curricular areas. Middle and secondary school teachers must demonstrate a high level of competency in all subject areas taught. Demonstration of subject-matter knowledge and competency may be shown by passing a state certification exam or licensing test in the relevant subject(s).

This report examines implementation of NCLB requirement and estimates the extent to which schools will achieve the goal of placing a highly qualified teacher in every classroom. After describing the highly qualified teacher requirement in detail, the report analyzes data from a national survey of schools that provide information on teacher qualifications and subjects taught. These data suggest that more than four out of five teachers would have met NCLB definition of a highly qualified teacher prior to the date of enactment.

The analysis also reveals differences between highly qualified and underqualified teachers — both in terms of the teachers' characteristics and the characteristics of the schools in which they teach. The findings have important implications for future policy-making in the area of teacher quality. The report concludes with a discussion of issues that may be considered as the Elementary and Secondary Education Act reauthorization process unfolds.

These provisions, along with the rest of the Elementary and Secondary Education Act, will likely be considered for reauthorization by the 110th Congress.

Chapter 6 - The No Child Left Behind Act of 2001 (NCLBA, P.L. 107-110) represents a major overhaul of federal programs for the education of limited English proficient and recent immigrant students. Programs for bilingual and immigrant education under the Elementary and Secondary Education Act of 1965 (ESEA) were consolidated and underwent several important changes with regard to the funding mechanism, method of instructional delivery, and focus on educational outcomes and accountability.

The NCLBA consolidated several competitively awarded grants in the Bilingual Education Act and a formula grant in the Emergency Immigrant Education Act (ESEA, Title VII, Parts A and C) into a single population-based formula grant. The new Language Acquisition State Formula Grant Program (ESEA, Title III) allocates 80% of funding according to the population of limited English proficient (LEP) students and 20% according to the population of recently arriving immigrants.

The law gives state and local educational agencies greater flexibility in the design and administration of language instructional programs and removes language in Title VII that encouraged bilingual instruction methods (i.e., curricula that develop proficiency in more than one language). At the same time, the law develops and focuses greater attention to the achievement of English proficiency.

Among many amendments to pupil assessment, the NCLBA builds upon language in the 1994 ESEA amendments. The law increases the reporting requirements for language and academic assessments as well as the accommodations under which those assessments are given to LEP pupils. Recipients of Title III money are also subjected to greater accountability standards tied to Title I adequate yearly progress (AYP) provisions.

In the first year of its existence, funding for Title III was dramatically increased over the previous year's Title VII appropriation — from $460 million in FY2001 to $665 million in FY2002. Since that time, the appropriations for the program have remained stable — $684 million in FY2003, $681 million in FY2004, $676 million in FY2005, and $669 million in FY2006.

Title III, along with the rest of the ESEA, will likely be considered for reauthorization by the 110th Congress.

Chapter 7 - Under the No Child Left Behind Act (NCLBA) of 2001, which amended the Elementary and Secondary Education Act (ESEA), high schools that receive federal funds must provide certain student contact information to military recruiters upon request and must allow recruiters to have the same access to students as employers and colleges. Because the 110th Congress is likely to consider reauthorization of the ESEA, legislators may contemplate changes to the military recruitment provisions, either as part of the reauthorization or as stand-alone legislation. Currently, one bill, H.R. 1346, has been introduced in the 110th Congress. This report describes the NCLBA military recruitment provisions and discusses the legal issues that they may raise.

When Congress enacted the No Child Left Behind Act (NCLBA) of 2001,[1] it added several new requirements regarding the ability of military recruiters to access student information and to approach students directly. These new provisions — which are different from similar Department of Defense (DOD) provisions that allow DOD to compile directory information on high school students for military recruitment purposes or that require colleges and universities that receive federal funds to allow military recruiters on campus[2] — have proven to be somewhat controversial. Proponents of the recruitment provisions argue that the new law allows recruiters to inform students about the military opportunities available to them and eases the task of recruiting volunteers to sustain the nation's military forces. On the other hand, opponents contend that the provisions raise concerns about student privacy and should be changed to make it easier to opt out.[3] Currently, 95% of the country's school districts are estimated to be complying with the new requirements,[4] although it is important to note that, traditionally, most schools had already allowed military recruiters to contact students long before the NCLBA provisions became mandatory.[5]

The new NCLBA military recruitment provisions require high schools that receive federal funds to meet two requirements. First, such schools must "provide, on a request made by military recruiters ..., access to secondary school students names, addresses, and telephone listings,"[6] and second, schools must "provide military recruiters the same access to secondary school students as is provided generally to post secondary educational institutions or to prospective employers of those students."[7] Schools that fail to comply with either of these two requirements — access to student information or equal access to students themselves — risk losing federal funds. However, private secondary schools that maintain a religious objection to military service are exempt from the recruitment provisions.[8]

Chapter 8 - The No Child Left Behind Act of 2001 (NCLBA) established minimum qualifications for paraprofessionals employed in Title I, Part A-funded schools. Paraprofessionals in such schools who perform instructional duties were required to meet these qualifications by the end of the 2005-2006 school year. This report describes the act's paraprofessional quality requirements and discusses their implementation and specification through guidance by the U.S. Department of Education. The report concludes with some issues that may arise as the 110th Congress considers reauthorization of the Elementary and Secondary Education Act of 1965 (ESEA).

In: No Child Left Behind: Issues and Developments
Editor: P. H. Berkhart, pp. 1-35
ISBN: 978-1-60456-210-1

Chapter 1

ADEQUATE YEARLY PROGRESS (AYP): IMPLEMENTATION OF THE NO CHILD LEFT BEHIND ACT*

Wayne C. Riddle

ABSTRACT

Title I, Part A of the Elementary and Secondary Education Act (ESEA), authorizes financial aid to local educational agencies (LEAs) for the education of disadvantaged children and youth at the preschool, elementary, and secondary levels. Over the last several years, the accountability provisions of this program have been increasingly focused on achievement and other outcomes for participating pupils and schools. Since 1994, and particularly under the No Child Left Behind Act of 2001 (NCLB), a key concept embodied in these requirements is that of "adequate yearly progress (AYP)" for schools, LEAs, and states. AYP is defined primarily on the basis of aggregate scores of various groups of pupils on state assessments of academic achievement. The primary purpose of AYP requirements is to serve as the basis for identifying schools and LEAs where performance is unsatisfactory, so that inadequacies may be addressed first through provision of increased support and, ultimately, a variety of "corrective actions."

Under NCLB, the Title I-A requirements for state-developed standards of AYP were substantially expanded in scope and specificity. Under NCLB, AYP calculations must be disaggregated — that is, determined separately and specifically for not only all pupils but also for several demographic groups of pupils within each school, LEA, and state. In addition, while AYP standards had to be applied previously only to pupils, schools, and LEAs participating in Title I-A, AYP standards under NCLB must be applied to *all* public schools, LEAs, and to states overall, if a state chooses to receive Title I-A grants. However, corrective actions for failing to meet AYP standards need be applied only to schools and LEAs participating in Title I-A. Another major break with the past is that state AYP standards must now incorporate concrete movement toward meeting an ultimate goal of all pupils reaching a proficient or advanced level of achievement by 2014.

---

* Excerpted from CRS Report RL32495, dated September 17, 2007.

The overall percentage of public schools identified as failing to make AYP for one or more years based on test scores in 2004-2005 was approximately 26% of *all* public schools. The percentage of schools for individual states varied from 2% to 66%. Approximately 14% of Title I-A participating schools were in the "needs improvement" status (i.e., they had failed to meet AYP standards for two or more consecutive years) based on AYP determinations for 2004-2005 and preceding school years.

The AYP provisions of NCLB are challenging and complex, and they have generated substantial interest and debate. Debates regarding NCLB provisions on AYP have focused on the provision for an ultimate goal, use of confidence intervals and data-averaging, population diversity effects, minimum pupil group size (n), separate focus on specific pupil groups, number of schools identified and state variations therein, the 95% participation rule, state variations in assessments and proficiency standards, and timing. ESEA programs are authorized through FY2008, and it is generally assumed that the 110th Congress will actively consider legislation to amend and extend the ESEA.

Background: Title I Outcome Accountability and the AYP Concept

Title I, Part A of the Elementary and Secondary Education Act (ESEA), the largest federal K-12 education program, authorizes financial aid to local educational agencies (LEAs) for the education of disadvantaged children and youth at the preschool, elementary, and secondary levels.

Since the 1988 reauthorization of the ESEA (The Augustus F. Hawkins-Robert T. Stafford Elementary and Secondary School Improvement Amendments of 1988, or "School Improvement Act," P.L. 100-297), the accountability provisions of this program have been increasingly focused on achievement and other outcomes for participating pupils and schools. Since the subsequent ESEA reauthorization in 1994 (the Improving America's Schools Act of 1994, P.L. 103-382), and particularly under the No Child Left Behind Act of 2001 (NCLB, P.L. 107-110), a key concept embodied in these outcome accountability requirements is that of "adequate yearly progress (AYP)" for schools, LEAs, and (more recently) states overall. The primary purpose of AYP requirements is to serve as the basis for identifying schools and LEAs where performance is inadequate, so that these inadequacies may be addressed, first through provision of increased support and, ultimately, through a variety of "corrective actions."[1]

This report is intended to provide an overview of the AYP concept and several related issues, a description of the AYP provisions of the No Child Left Behind Act, and an analysis of the implementation of these provisions by the U.S. Department of Education (ED) and the states. ESEA programs are authorized through FY2008, and it is generally assumed that the 110th Congress will actively consider legislation to amend and extend the ESEA.

General Elements of AYP Provisions

ESEA Title I, Part A has included requirements for participating LEAs and states to administer assessments of academic achievement to participating pupils, and to evaluate LEA programs at least every two years, since the program was initiated in 1965. However, relatively little attention was paid to school- or LEA-wide outcome accountability until adoption of the School Improvement Act of 1988.[2] Under the School Improvement Act, requirements for states and LEAs to evaluate the performance of Title I-A schools and individual participating pupils were expanded. In addition, LEAs and states were for the first time required to develop and implement improvement plans for pupils and schools whose performance was not improving. However, in comparison to current Title I-A outcome accountability provisions, these requirements were broad and vague. States and LEAs were given little direction as to how they were to determine whether performance was satisfactory, or how performance was to be defined, with one partial exception.

The exception applied to schools conducting schoolwide programs under Title I-A. In schoolwide programs, Title I-A funds may be used to improve instruction for all pupils in the school, rather than being targeted on only the lowest-achieving individual pupils in the school (as under the other major Title I-A service model, targeted assistance schools). Under the 1988 version of the ESEA, schoolwide programs were limited to schools where 75% or more of the pupils were from low-income families (currently this threshold has been reduced to 40%). The School Improvement Act required schoolwide programs, in order to maintain their special authority, to demonstrate that the academic achievement of pupils in the school was higher than either of the following: (a) the average level of achievement for pupils participating in Title I-A in the LEA overall; or (b) the average level of achievement for disadvantaged pupils enrolled in that school during the three years preceding schoolwide program implementation.

The embodiment of outcome accountability in the specific concept of AYP began with the 1994 Improving America's Schools Act (IASA). Under the IASA, states participating in Title I-A were required to develop AYP standards as a basis for systematically determining whether schools and LEAs receiving Title I-A grants were performing at an acceptable level. Failure to meet the state AYP standards was to become the basis for directing technical assistance, and ultimately corrective actions, toward schools and LEAs where performance was consistently unacceptable.

Generic AYP Factors

Before proceeding to a description of the Title I-A AYP provisions under the IASA of 1994, we outline below the general types of major provisions frequently found in AYP provisions, actual or proposed.

Primary Basis

They are based primarily on aggregate measures of academic achievement by pupils. As long as Title I-A has contained AYP provisions, it has provided that these be based ultimately on state standards of curriculum content and pupil performance, and assessments linked to these standards. More specifically, the Title I-A requirements have been focused on the percentage of pupils scoring at the "proficient" or higher level of achievement on state assessments, not a common national standard. However, when AYP provisions were first adopted in 1994, states were given an extended period of time to adopt and implement these standards and assessments, and for a lengthy period after the 1994 amendments, various "transitional" performance standards and assessments were used to measure academic achievement.[3]

Ultimate Goal

AYP standards may or may not incorporate an ultimate goal, which may be relatively specific and demanding (e.g., all pupils should reach the proficient or higher level of achievement, as defined by each state, in a specified number of years), or more ambiguous and less demanding (e.g., pupil achievement levels must increase in relation to either LEA or state averages or past performance). If there is a specific ultimate goal, there may also be requirements for specific, numerical, annual objectives either for pupils in the aggregate or for each of several pupil groups. The primary purpose of such a goal is to require that levels of achievement continuously increase over time in order to be considered satisfactory.

Subject Areas

With respect to subject areas, AYP standards might focus only on reading and math achievement, or they might include additional subject areas.

Additional Indicators

In addition to pupil scores on assessments, AYP standards often include one or more supplemental indicators, which may or may not be academic. Examples include high school graduation rates, attendance rates, or assessment scores in subjects other than those that are required.

Levels at Which Applied

States may be required to develop AYP standards for, and apply them to, schools, LEAs, and/or for states overall. Further, it may be required that AYP standards be applicable to *all* schools and LEAs, or only to those participating in ESEA Title I-A.

Disaggregation of Pupil Groups

AYP standards might be applied simply to all pupils in a school, LEA, or state, or they might also be applied separately and specifically to a variety of demographic groups of pupils — such as economically disadvantaged pupils, pupils with disabilities, pupils in different ethnic or racial groups, or limited English proficient pupils. In a program such as Title I-A, the purpose of which is to improve education for the disadvantaged, it may be especially important to consider selected disadvantaged pupil groups separately, to identify situations where overall pupil achievement may be satisfactory, but the performance of one or more disadvantaged pupil groups is not.

Basic Structure

The basic structure of AYP Models generally falls into one of three general categories. The three basic structural forms for AYP of schools or LEAs are the *group status*, *successive group improvement*, and *individual/cohort growth* models. In the context of these terms, "group" (or "subgroup," in the case of detailed demographic categories) refers to a collection of pupils that is identified by their grade level and usually other demographic characteristics (e.g., race, ethnicity, or educational disadvantage) as of a point in time. The actual pupils in a "group" may change substantially, or even completely, from one year to the next. In contrast, a "cohort" refers to a collection of pupils in which the same pupils are followed from year to year.

The key characteristic of the group status model is a required threshold level of achievement that is the same for all pupil groups, schools, and LEAs statewide in a given subject and grade level. Under this model, performance at a point in time is compared to a benchmark at that time, with no direct consideration of changes over a previous period and whatever the school's or LEA's "starting point." For example, it might be required that 45% or more of the pupils in any of a state's elementary schools score at the proficient or higher level of achievement in order for a school to make AYP. "Status" models emphasize the importance of meeting certain minimum levels of achievement for all pupil groups, schools, and LEAs, and arguably apply consistent expectations to all.

The key characteristic of the successive group improvement model is a focus on the rate of change in achievement in a subject area from one year to the next among groups of pupils in a grade level at a school or LEA (e.g., the percentage of this year's 5th grade pupils in a school who are at a proficient or higher level in mathematics compared to the percentage of last year's 5th grade pupils who were at a proficient or higher level of achievement).

Finally, the key characteristic of the individual/cohort growth model is a focus on the rate of change over time in the level of achievement among cohorts of the same pupils. Growth models are longitudinal, based upon the tracking of the same pupils as they progress through their K-12 education careers. While the progress of pupils is tracked individually, results are typically aggregated when used for accountability purposes. Aggregation may be by demographic group, by school or LEA, or other relevant characteristics. In general, growth models would give credit for meeting steps along the way to proficiency in ways that a status model typically does not.

Alternative or "Safe Harbor" Provisions

AYP systems often have alternative provisions under which schools or LEAs that fail to meet the usual requirements may still be deemed to have made AYP if they meet certain specified alternative conditions. For example, under a status model, it might be generally required that 45% or more of the pupils in any of a state's elementary schools score at the proficient or higher level of achievement in order for the school to make AYP, but a school where aggregate achievement is below this level might still be deemed to have made AYP, through a "safe harbor" provision, if the percentage of pupils at the proficient or higher level in the school is higher than for the previous year by some specified degree. Such a concept may be seen as adding a successive group improvement model element to a status model of AYP.

Assessment Participation Rate

It might be required that a specified minimum percentage of a school's or LEA's pupils participate in assessments in order for the school or LEA to be deemed to have met AYP standards. The primary purposes of such a requirement are to assure that assessment results are broadly representative of the achievement level of the school's pupils, and to minimize the incentives for school staff to discourage test participation by pupils deemed likely to perform poorly on assessments.

Exclusion of Certain Pupils

Beyond general participation rate requirements (see above), states may be specifically required to include, or allowed to exclude, certain groups of pupils in determining whether schools or LEAs meet AYP requirements. For example, statutory provisions might allow the exclusion of pupils who have attended a school for less than one year in determining whether a school meets AYP standards.

Special Provisions for Pupils with Particular Educational Needs

Beyond requirements that all pupils be included in assessments, with accommodations where appropriate, there may be special provisions for limited English proficient (LEP) pupils or pupils with the most significant cognitive disabilities.

Averaging or Other Statistical Manipulation of Data

Finally, there are a variety of ways in which statistical manipulation of AYP-related data or calculations might be either authorized or prohibited. Major possibilities include averaging of test score data over periods of two or more years, rather than use of the latest data in all cases; or the use of "confidence intervals" in calculating whether the aggregate performance of a school's pupils is at the level specified by the state's AYP standards. These techniques, and the implications of their use, are discussed further below. In general, their use tends to improve the reliability and validity of AYP determinations, while often reducing the number of schools or LEAs identified as failing to meet AYP standards.

AYP Provisions under the IASA of 1994

Under the IASA, states were to develop and implement AYP standards soon after enactment. However, states were given several years (generally until the 2000-2001 school year) to develop and implement curriculum content standards, pupil performance standards, and assessments linked to these for at least three grade levels in math and reading.[4] Thus, during the period between adoption of the IASA in 1994 and of NCLB in early 2002, for most states the AYP provisions were based on "transitional" assessments and pupil performance standards that were widely varying in nature. AYP standards based on such "transitional" assessments were considered to be "transitional" themselves, with "final" AYP standards to be based on states' "final" assessments, when implemented. The subject areas required to be included in state AYP standards (as opposed to required assessments) were not explicitly specified in statute; ED policy guidance required states to include only math and reading achievement in determining AYP. Further, the inclusion in AYP standards of measures other than academic achievement in math and reading on state assessments was optional.

With respect to the ultimate goal of the state AYP standards, the IASA provided broadly that there must be continuous and substantial progress toward a goal of having all pupils meet the proficient and advanced levels of achievement. However, no timeline was specified for reaching this goal, and most states did not incorporate it into their AYP plans in any concrete way.

The IASA's AYP standards were to be applied to schools and LEAs, but not to the states overall. Further, while states were encouraged to apply the AYP standards to *all* public schools and LEAs, states could choose to apply them only to schools and LEAs participating in Title I-A, and most did so limit their application.

The IASA provided that all relevant pupils[5] were to be included in assessments and AYP determinations, although assessments were to include results for pupils who had attended a school for less than one year only in tabulating LEA-wide results (i.e., not for individual schools). LEP pupils were to be assessed in the language that would best reflect their knowledge of subjects other than English; and accommodations were to be provided to pupils with disabilities.

Importantly, while the IASA required state assessments to ultimately (by 2000-2001) provide test results that were disaggregated by pupil demographic groups, it did not require such disaggregation of data in AYP standards and calculations. The 1994 statute provided that state AYP standards must consider all pupils, "particularly" economically disadvantaged and LEP pupils, but did not specify that the AYP definition must be based on each of these pupil groups separately. Finally, the statute was silent with respect to data-averaging or other statistical techniques, as well as the basic structure of state AYP standards (i.e., whether a "group status," "successive group improvement," or "individual/cohort growth" model must be employed).

Concerns About the AYP Provisions of the IASA

Thus, the IASA's provisions for state AYP standards broke new ground conceptually, but were comparatively broad and ambiguous. While states were required to adopt and implement at least "transitional" AYP standards, based on "transitional" state assessment results, soon after enactment of the IASA, they were not required to adopt "final" AYP standards, in conjunction with final assessments and pupil performance standards, until the 2000-2001 school year. Further, states were not allowed to implement most corrective actions, such as reconstituting school staff, until they adopted final assessments, so these provisions were not implemented by most states until the IASA was replaced by NCLB.

A compilation was prepared by the Consortium for Policy Research in Education (CPRE) of the "transitional" AYP standards that states were applying in administering their Title I-A programs during the 1999-2000 school year.[6] Overall, according to this compilation, the state AYP definitions for 1999-2000 were widely varied and frequently complex. General patterns in these AYP standards, outlined below, reflect state interpretation of the IASA's statutory requirements.

- Most considered only achievement test scores, but some considered a variety of additional factors, most often dropout rates or attendance rates.
- Often, the state AYP standards set a threshold of some minimum percentage, or minimum rate of increase in the percentage, of pupils at the proficient or higher level of achievement on a composite of state tests. These thresholds were often based, at least in part, on performance of pupils in a school or LEA relative to statewide averages or to the school's or the LEA's performance in the previous year. Several states identified schools as failing to make AYP if they fail to meet "expected growth" in performance based on factors such as initial achievement levels and statewide average achievement trends. These thresholds almost never incorporated a "ladder" of movement toward an ultimate goal of all pupils at the proficient level, or otherwise explicitly incorporated an ultimate goal to be met by some specific date.
- While some state AYP standards were based on achievement results for a single year, they were frequently based on two- or three-year rolling averages.
- The AYP standards generally referred only to all pupils in a school or LEA combined, without a specific focus on any pupil demographic groups. However, the

AYP standards of some states included a focus on a single category of low-achieving pupils separately from all pupils, and a very few (e.g., Texas) included a specific focus on the performance of several pupil groups (African American, Hispanic, White, or Economically Disadvantaged). One state (New Mexico) compared school scores to predicted scores based on such factors as pupil demographics.

- The state AYP standards under the IASA were sometimes substantially adjusted from year-to-year (often with consequent wide variations in the percentage of Title I-A schools identified as needing improvement). According to CPRE, two states (Iowa and New Hampshire) left AYP standards and determinations almost totally to individual LEAs in 1999-2000.

A report published by ED in 2004, based on state AYP policies for the 2001-2002 school year, contains similar conclusions about state AYP policies in the period immediately preceding implementation of NCLB.[7] There was tremendous variation among the states in the impact of their AYP policies under the IASA on the number and percentage of Title I-A schools and LEAs that were identified as failing to meet the AYP standards. In some states, a substantial majority of Title I-A schools were identified as failing to make AYP, while in others almost no schools were so identified. In July 2002, just before the initial implementation of the new AYP provisions of NCLB, ED released a compilation of the number of schools identified as failing to meet AYP standards for two or more consecutive years (and therefore identified as being in need of improvement) in 2001-2002 (for most states) or 2000-2001 (in states where 2001-2002 data were not available).[8] The national total number of these schools was 8,652; the number in individual states ranged from zero in Arkansas and Wyoming to 1,513 in Michigan and 1,009 in California.[9] While there are obvious differences in the size of these states, there were also wide variations in the percentage of all schools participating in Title I-A that failed to meet AYP for either one year or two or more consecutive years.

AYP under NCLB Statute

NCLB provisions regarding AYP may be seen as an evolution of, and to a substantial degree as a reaction to perceived weaknesses in, the AYP requirements of the 1994 IASA. The latter were frequently criticized as being insufficiently specific, detailed, or challenging. Criticism often focused specifically on their failure to focus on specific disadvantaged pupil groups, failure to require continuous improvement toward an ultimate goal, and their required applicability only to schools and LEAs participating in Title I-A, not to all public schools or to states overall.

Under NCLB, the Title I-A requirements for state-developed standards of AYP were substantially expanded in scope and specificity. As under the IASA, AYP is defined primarily on the basis of aggregate scores of pupils on state assessments of academic achievement. However, under NCLB, state AYP standards must also include at least one additional academic indicator, which in the case of high schools must be the graduation rate. The additional indicators may not be employed in a way that would reduce the number of schools or LEAs identified as failing to meet AYP standards.[10]

One of the most important differences between AYP standards under NCLB and previous requirements is that under NCLB, AYP calculations must be disaggregated — that is, they must be determined separately and specifically for not only all pupils but also for several demographic groups of pupils within each school, LEA, and state. Test scores for an individual pupil may be taken into consideration multiple times, depending on the number of designated groups of which they are a member (e.g., a pupil might be considered as part of the LEP and economically disadvantaged groups, as well as the "all pupils" group). The specified demographic groups are as follows:

- economically disadvantaged pupils,
- LEP pupils,
- pupils with disabilities, and
- pupils in major racial and ethnic groups, as well as all pupils.

However, as is discussed further below, there are three major constraints on the consideration of these pupil groups in AYP calculations. First, pupil groups need not be considered in cases where their number is so relatively small that achievement results would not be statistically significant or the identity of individual pupils might be divulged.[11] As is discussed further below, the selection of the minimum number (n) of pupils in a group for the group to be considered in AYP determinations has been left largely to state discretion. State policies regarding "n" have varied widely, with important implications for the number of pupil groups actually considered in making AYP determinations for many schools and LEAs, and the number of schools or LEAs potentially identified as failing to make AYP. Second, it has been left to the states to define the "major racial and ethnic groups" on the basis of which AYP must be calculated. And third, as under the IASA, pupils who have not attended the same school for a full year need not be considered in determining AYP for the school, although they are still to be included in LEA and state AYP determinations.

In contrast to the previous statute, under which AYP standards had to be applied only to pupils, schools, and LEAs participating in Title I-A, AYP standards under NCLB must be applied to *all* public schools, LEAs, and for the first time to states overall, if a state chooses to receive Title I-A grants. However, corrective actions for failing to meet AYP standards need only be applied to schools and LEAs participating in Title I-A.

Another major break with the past is that state AYP standards must now incorporate concrete movement toward meeting an ultimate goal of all pupils reaching a proficient or advanced level of achievement within 12 years (the 2013-2014 school year). The steps — that is, required levels of achievement — toward meeting this goal must increase in "equal increments" over time. The first increase in the thresholds must occur after no more than two years, and remaining increases at least once every three years. As is discussed further below, several states have accommodated this requirement in ways that require much more rapid progress in the later years of the period leading up to 2013-2014 than in the earlier period.

The primary basic structure for AYP under NCLB is now specified in the authorizing statute as a group status model. A "uniform bar" approach is employed: states are to set a threshold percentage of pupils at proficient or advanced levels each year that is applicable to all pupil subgroups of sufficient size to be considered in AYP determinations. The threshold levels of achievement are to be set separately for reading and math, and may be set separately for each level of K-12 education (elementary, middle, and high schools). The minimum[12] starting point for the "uniform bar" in the initial period is to be the greater of (a) the percentage of pupils at the proficient or advanced level of achievement for the lowest-achieving pupil group in the base year,[13] *or* (b) the percentage of pupils at the proficient or advanced level of achievement for the lowest-performing quintile (fifth)[14] of schools statewide in the base year.[15] The "uniform bar" must generally be increased at least once every three years, although in the initial period it must be increased after no more than two years.

In determining whether scores for a group of pupils are at the required level, the averaging of scores over two to three years is allowed. In addition, NCLB includes a safe harbor provision, under which a school that does not meet the standard AYP requirements may still be deemed to meet AYP if it experiences a 10% (not a 10 percentage point) reduction in the gap between 100% and the base year for the specific pupil groups that fail to meet the "uniform bar," and those pupil groups make progress on at least one other academic indicator included in the state's AYP standards. As noted earlier, this alternative provision adds successive group improvement as a secondary AYP model under NCLB. In addition, as is discussed below, under a pilot project, seven states have been approved to use a third model of AYP — a "growth model" — for AYP determinations.

Finally, NCLB AYP provisions include an assessment participation rate requirement. In order for a school to meet AYP standards, at least 95% of all pupils, as well as at least 95% of each of the demographic groups of pupils considered for AYP determinations for the school or LEA, must participate in the assessments that serve as the primary basis for AYP determinations.[16]

ED Regulations and Guidance on Implementation of the AYP Provisions of NCLB

States began determining AYP for schools, LEAs, and the states overall based on NCLB provisions beginning with the 2002-2003 school year. The deadline for states to submit to ED their AYP standards based on NCLB provisions was January 31, 2003, and according to ED, all states met this deadline. On June 10, 2003, ED announced that accountability plans had been approved for all states. However, many of the approved plans required states to take additional actions following submission of their plan.[17]

In the period preceding ED's review of state accountability plans under NCLB, the Department published two relevant documents. Regulations, published in the *Federal Register* on December 2, 2002, mirrored the detailed provisions in the authorizing statute. The second document, a policy letter published by the Secretary of Education on July 24, 2002,[18] emphasized flexibility, stating that "The purpose of the statute, for both assessments and accountability, is to build on high quality accountability systems that States already have in place, not to require every state to start from scratch." The letter went on to list 10 criteria that it said would be applied by ED in the process of reviewing state AYP standards. These criteria included most, but not all, of the specifications regarding AYP from the authorizing statute and regulations (e.g., applicability to all public schools and their pupils, and specific focus on individual pupil groups). In response to concerns that large numbers of schools might be identified as failing to make AYP (as is discussed further below), ED officials emphasized the importance of taking action to identify and move to improve underperforming schools, no matter how numerous. They also emphasized the possibilities for flexibility and variation in taking corrective actions with respect to schools that fail to meet AYP, depending on the extent to which they fail to meet those standards.

Aspects of state AYP plans that apparently received special attention in ED's reviews included (1) the pace at which proficiency levels are expected to improve (e.g., equal increments of improvement over the entire period, or much more rapid improvement expected in later years than at the beginning); (2) whether schools or LEAs must fail to meet AYP with respect to the same pupil group(s), grade level(s) and/or subject areas to be identified as needing improvement, or whether two consecutive years of failure to meet AYP with respect to *any* of these categories should lead to identification;[19] (3) the length of time over which pupils should be identified as being LEP; (4) the minimum size of pupil groups in a school in order for the group to be considered in AYP determinations or for reporting of scores; (5) whether to allow schools credit for raising pupil scores from below basic to basic (as well as from basic or below to proficient or above) in making AYP determinations; and (6) whether to allow use of statistical techniques such as "confidence intervals" (i.e., whether scores are below the required level to a statistically significant extent) in AYP determinations.

Recent Developments

On April 7, 2005, the Secretary of Education met with a group of chief state school officers and announced a new, more flexible approach on AYP policies.[20] This announcement followed a number of instances, beginning in late 2003, in which ED officials published additional regulations and other policy guidance on selected aspects of AYP determination and related assessment issues, in an effort to provide additional flexibility. This guidance has addressed several aspects of AYP implementation that have created particular difficulties for many schools and LEAs: assessment participation rates, calculation of AYP with respect to LEP pupils and pupils with disabilities, plus options for determining AYP in targeted assistance Title I-A programs. While all of these new forms of flexibility may clearly be employed in making future AYP determinations, it is ED's position that they may not be applied retroactively to AYP determinations for years preceding the time when each particular form of flexibility is announced.[21]

At the same time, it has been widely reported that one state has been fined by ED for failure to publish AYP results for schools in a timely manner. According to articles published by these sources in April 2005, the Texas SEA has been fined $444,282 in Title I-A state administration funds for failure to release AYP results, based on assessment scores for the 2003-2004 school year, until September 30, 2004.[22]

Growth Model Pilot

In November 2005, the Secretary of Education announced a growth model pilot program under which up to 10 states would be allowed to use growth models to make AYP determinations for the 2005-2006 or subsequent school years.[23] The models proposed by the states must meet at least the following criteria (in addition to a variety of criteria applicable to all state AYP policies — that is, measure achievement separately in reading/language arts and mathematics):

- they must incorporate an ultimate goal of all pupils reaching a proficient or higher level of achievement by the end of the 2013- 2014 school year;

- achievement gaps among pupil groups must decline in order for schools or LEAs to meet AYP standards;
- annual achievement goals for pupils must not be set on the basis of pupil background or school characteristics;
- annual achievement goals must be based on performance standards, not past or "typical" performance growth rates;
- the assessment system must produce comparable results from grade-to-grade and year-to-year; and
- the progress of individual students must be tracked within a state data system.

In addition, applicant states must have their annual assessments for each of grades 3-8 approved by ED, and these assessments must have been in place for at least one year previous to implementation of the growth models.

In January 2006, ED published peer review guidance for growth model pilot applications.[24] In general, this guidance elaborates upon the requirements described above, with special emphasis on the following: (a) pupil growth targets may not consider their "race/ethnicity, socioeconomic status, school AYP status, or any other non-academic" factor; (b) growth targets are to be established on the basis of achievement standards, not typical growth patterns or past achievement; and (c) the state must have a longitudinal, individual pupil data system, capable of tracking pupils as they move among schools and LEAs within the state.

The requirements for growth models of AYP under this pilot are relatively restrictive. The models must be consistent with the ultimate goal of all pupils at a proficient or higher level by 2013-2014, a major goal of the statutory AYP provisions of NCLB. More significantly, they must incorporate comparable annual assessments, at least for each of grades 3-8 plus at least one senior high school year, and those assessments must be approved by ED and in place for at least one year before implementation of the growth model. Further, all performance expectations must be individualized, and the state must have an infrastructure of a statewide, longitudinal database for individual pupils. Proposed models would have to be structured around expectations and performance of individual pupils, not demographic groups of pupils in a school or LEA, although individual results would have to be aggregated for the demographic groups designated in NCLB.

According to ED, 20 states submitted applications to be allowed to use growth models to make AYP determinations beginning with either the 2005-2006 or 2006-2007 school years. Two states, North Carolina and Tennessee, were initially approved to use proposed growth models in making AYP determinations based on assessments administered in the 2005-2006 school year. Seven additional states —Arkansas, Delaware, Florida, Iowa, Ohio, Alaska, and Arizona — have been approved to participate in the pilot program subsequently, contingent in the case of hio on adoption of a uniform minimum group size for all pupil groups. The models for these nine states are briefly described below.

The North Carolina policy does not actually provide for a separate AYP model, but rather the addition of a projection component to the current group status model. If the achievement level of a non-proficient pupil is on a trajectory toward proficiency within four years, then the pupil is added to the proficient group. All other provisions of the current group status and successive group improvement models would continue to apply. Thus, the ultimate goal becomes: by the end of the 2013-2014 school year, all pupils will be either at a proficient or higher level, or on a four-year trajectory toward proficiency (without use of confidence intervals). The trajectory calculations will be made for pupils in the 3rd through 8th grades. SEA staff estimate that 4% of the schools in North Carolina that failed to meet AYP standards based on 2004-2005 assessment results would have met AYP standards if this growth model had been in place.

Under the Tennessee policy, schools and LEAs will have two options for meeting AYP: meeting either the AYP standards under the group status or successive group improvement models of current law, or meeting AYP standards according to a "projection model." Under the projection model, pupils are deemed to be at a proficient or higher level of achievement if their test scores are projected to be at a proficient or higher level three years into the future, based on past achievement levels for individual pupils. It should be noted that under this model, pupils who currently score at a proficient level, but who would be projected to score below a proficient level in three years, would not be counted as proficient. Further, the Tennessee growth/projection model implicitly assumes that pupils attend schools performing at a state average level. If, in actuality, they attend low-performing schools, their future achievement level may be overestimated.

Tennessee's projection model will not be applied to high schools. SEA staff estimate that 13% of the schools in Tennessee that failed to meet AYP standards based on 2004-2005 assessment results would have met AYP standards if this model had been in place.

Under the Delaware growth model, AYP will be calculated each year based on both the statutory provisions and using the state's growth model. A school will meet AYP standards if it qualifies using either method. Individual pupil performance will be tracked from one year to the next. Specified numbers of points (up to 300) will be awarded based on changes (if any) in pupils' performance level. Points will be awarded for partial movement toward proficiency, but the points awarded for movement to advanced levels beyond proficiency will be the same as for movement to proficiency. (Maintaining a level of proficient or higher awards 300 points as well.) The average growth scores for schools and LEAs to meet AYP standards increase steadily until 2013-2014, by which time all pupils would be expected to achieve at a proficient or higher level.[25]

Under the Arkansas policy, AYP will be calculated each year based on both statutory provisions and using the state's growth model. A school will meet AYP standards if it qualifies using either method. Under the growth model, pupils in grades 4-8 will be deemed to be proficient if they are on a growth path toward proficiency by the end of 8th grade. Pupils already proficient must be on a path to continue to be proficient through grade 8 (i.e., growth path criteria will be applied to all pupils, proficient and non-proficient). Individual annual proficiency thresholds and growth increments are designed to enable non-proficient students to reach proficiency by grade 8, and proficient students to continue to be proficient. Mobile pupils will be associated with the school they attended at the time of assessment administration in the previous year.

Under the Florida model, AYP will be determined separately for each pupil subgroup in each school or LEA (i.e., not for schools or LEAs as a whole) using the statutory models (status and safe harbor) plus a growth model. The school or LEA will meet AYP standards if each pupil subgroup makes AYP using one of the three models.

Florida's growth model will be essentially the same as the current status model, except that proficient pupils will include both those currently scoring at a proficient or higher level plus those who are on an individual path toward proficiency within three years. The combined percentage of pupils rated proficient will be compared to the standard AMO. The model will be applied to AYP determinations for grades 3-10 (with some modifications for pupils in grade 3). In its application, the Florida SEA estimated that for 2006-2007, 938 of the state's public schools would meet AYP standards with the growth model applied, compared to 743 schools without (out of a total of 3,200 schools).

Under the Iowa model, pupil tests score ranges below proficient have been divided into 3 categories: Hi Marginal, Lo Marginal, and Weak. A student who rises from one of these levels to a higher level, and has not previously attained the higher level, will be deemed to have met "Adequate Yearly Growth" (AYG). AYG is considered to be more than a typical year's growth over a one-year period. For schools and LEAs that have not met AYP though application of the standard status and safe harbor models, students making AYG will be added to those scoring proficient or above, and this combined total will be used in determining whether the school or LEA makes AYP for the year. Students scoring below the proficient level must continue to move to a higher sub-proficient level each year in order to be included in the combined proficient + AYG student count. This implies that students beginning at the Weak level must reach proficiency within three years, those beginning at Lo Marginal must become proficient within two years, and those beginning at Hi Marginal must reach proficiency within one year. By 2014, the growth model would no longer be used, and all pupils will be expected to achieve at a proficient or higher level.

Confidence intervals will continue to be applied to determine whether the combined proficient + AYG student count meets the required threshold to make AYP. This growth model will be applied statewide to test scores for grades 3-8 and 11, and to grades 9 and 10 as well in the LEAs that administer the Iowa Tests in those grades. The Iowa growth model does not currently include students with the most significant cognitive disabilities, who take the Iowa Alternate Assessment.

Ohio has adopted a variation of the "projection" or "on track to proficiency" approach that is common to the models for all of the other participating states except Delaware and Iowa. After application of the standard status and safe harbor models, if any pupil group fails to meet AYP, then a determination will be made if a sufficient proportion of pupils in the group is on track toward meeting the required proficiency threshold as of a "target grade." In the case of elementary and middle schools, the target grade will be either the grade level following the highest grade offered by the school (i.e., for a K-5 school, the 6th grade), or 4 grades beyond the pupil's current grade, whichever comes first. In the case of a high school, pupils would have to be on track toward proficiency by the 11th grade.

Pupils currently scoring at a proficient level but who are projected to be below the proficient level by the target grade will not be considered to be proficient in Ohio's projection model. Student achievement trajectories will be projected on an individual basis. Projections will be based on past test results (in all subjects, but with greater weight applied to past test results in the same subject) for each pupil.

Under Alaska's growth model, pupils will be included in the proficient group if their achievement level trajectory is on a growth path toward proficiency within 3 additional years for pupils in grades 4-9, or within 2 additional years for pupils in grade 10. (Alaska currently has no standards-based assessments for grades beyond 10.) Pupils in the third grade (the earliest grade at which state assessments are administered) will be measured based on status only, not growth. The growth model will not apply to pupils with disabilities who take alternate assessments. While Alaska had proposed that confidence intervals be applied, at a relatively low level (68%), under the growth model, the state agreed to drop this in the approved version. In its application, Alaska estimated that approximately 13% of pupils currently not proficient are on track toward proficiency, under the terms of the state's growth model.

Finally, in Arizona, the growth model will be applicable to pupils in grades 4-8 only. Pupils will be included in the proficient group if their achievement level trajectory is on a growth path toward proficiency within three years or by 8th grade, whichever comes first. Pupils in the third grade (the earliest grade at which state assessments are administered) will be measured based on status only, not growth. Unlike some other states participating in the growth model pilot, pupils with disabilities who take the state's alternate assessment (AIMS-A) will be included in the Arizona growth model. Such pupils with disabilities who move up one performance level (i.e., from "falls far below" to "approaches" or from "approaches" to "meets" the proficiency standard) will be deemed to have met their growth target.

Thus, most of the growth models approved under ED's pilot programs are based upon supplementing the number of pupils scoring at a proficient or higher level with those who are projected to be at a proficient level within a limited number of years. Seven of the nine approved models follow this general approach. Among these states, a distinction may be made between five states (North Carolina, Arkansas, Florida, Alaska, and Arizona) that combine currently proficient pupils with those not proficient who are "on track" toward proficiency, and two states (Tennessee and Ohio) that consider only projected proficiency levels for all pupils (i.e., currently proficient pupils who are not on track to remain proficient are counted as not proficient). In contrast, the models used by the other two states — Delaware and Iowa — focus on awarding credit for movement of pupils among achievement categories up to proficiency.

Pupils with Disabilities

The most substantial of ED's recent AYP policy changes involves pupils with disabilities. First, regulations addressing the application of the Title I-A standards and assessment requirements to certain pupils with disabilities were published in the *Federal Register* on December 9, 2003 (pp. 68698-68708). The purpose of these regulations is to clarify the application of standard, assessment, and accountability provisions to pupils "with the most significant cognitive disabilities." Under the regulations, states and LEAs may adopt alternate assessments based on alternate achievement standards — aligned with the state's academic content standards and reflecting "professional judgment of the highest achievement standards possible" — for a limited percentage of pupils with disabilities.[26] The number of pupils whose proficient or higher scores on these alternate assessments may be considered as proficient or above for AYP purposes is limited to a maximum of 1.0% of all tested pupils (approximately 9% of all pupils with disabilities) at the state and LEA level (there is no limit for individual schools). SEAs may request from the U.S. Secretary of Education an exception allowing them to exceed the 1.0% cap statewide, and SEAs may grant such exceptions to LEAs within their state. According to ED staff, three states in 2003-2004 (Montana, Ohio, and Virginia), and four states in 2004-2005 (the preceding three states plus South Dakota), received waivers to go marginally above the 1.0% limit statewide. In the absence of a waiver, the number of pupils scoring at the "proficient or higher" level on alternate assessments, based on alternate achievement standards, in excess of the 1.0% limit is to be added to those scoring "below proficient" in LEA or state-level AYP determinations.

A new ED policy affecting an additional group of pupils with disabilities was announced initially in April 2005, with final regulations based on it published in the *Federal Register* on April 9, 2007. The new policy is divided into short-term and long-term phases. It is focused on pupils with disabilities whose ability to perform academically is assumed to be greater than that of the pupils with "the most significant cognitive disabilities" discussed in the above paragraph, and who are capable of achieving high standards, but may not reach grade level within the same time period as their peers. In ED's terminology, these pupils would be assessed using alternate assessments based on modified achievement standards.

The short-term policy may apply, with the approval of the Secretary, to states until they develop and administer alternative assessments under the long-term policy (described below).[27] Under this short-term policy, in eligible states that have not yet adopted modified achievement standards, schools may add to their proficient pupil group a number of pupils with disabilities equal to 2.0% of all pupils assessed (in effect, deeming the scores of all of these pupils to be at the proficient level).[28] This policy would be applicable only to schools and LEAs that would otherwise fail meet AYP standards due solely to their pupils with disabilities group. According to ED staff, as of the date of this report, 28 states are currently exercising this flexibility. Alternatively, in eligible states that have adopted modified achievement standards (currently six states), schools and LEAs may count proficient scores for pupils with disabilities on these assessments, subject to a 2.0% (of all assessed pupils) cap at the LEA and state levels.

The long-term policy is embodied in final regulations published in the *Federal Register* on April 9, 2007. These regulations affect standards, assessments, and AYP for a group of pupils with disabilities who are unlikely to achieve grade level proficiency within the current school year, but who are not among those pupils with the most significant cognitive disabilities (whose situation was addressed by an earlier set of regulations, discussed above). For this second group of pupils with disabilities, states would be authorized to develop "modified academic achievement standards" and alternate assessments linked to these. The modified achievement standards must be aligned with grade-level content standards, but may reflect reduced breadth or depth of grade-level content in comparison to the achievement standards applicable to the majority of pupils. The standards must provide access to grade-level curriculum, and not preclude affected pupils from earning a regular high school diploma.

As with the previous regulations regarding pupils with the most significant cognitive disabilities, there would be no direct limit on the number of pupils who take alternate assessments based on modified achievement standards. However, in AYP determinations, pupil scores of proficient or advanced on alternate assessments based on modified achievement standards may be counted only as long as they do not exceed a number equal to 2.0% of all pupils tested at the state or LEA level (i.e., an estimated 20% of pupils with disabilities); such scores in excess of the limit would be considered "non-proficient." As with the 1.0% cap for pupils with the most significant cognitive disabilities, this 2.0% cap does not apply to individual schools. In general, LEAs or states could exceed the 2.0% cap only if they did not reach the 1.0% limit with respect to pupils with the most significant cognitive disabilities. Thus, in general, scores of proficient or above on alternate assessments based on alternate *and* modified achievement standards may not exceed a total of 3.0% of all pupils tested at a state or LEA level.[29] In particular, states are no longer allowed to request a waiver of the 1.0% cap regarding pupils with the most significant cognitive disabilities.

The April 9, 2007, proposed regulations also include provisions that are widely applicable to AYP determinations. First, states are no longer allowed to use varying minimum group sizes ("n") for different demographic groups of pupils. This prohibits the previously common practice of setting higher "n" sizes for pupils with disabilities or LEP pupils than for other pupil groups. Second, when pupils take state assessments multiple times, states and LEAs may use the highest score for pupils who take tests more than once. Finally, as with LEP pupils, states and LEAs may include the test scores of former pupils with disabilities in the disability subgroup for up to two years after such pupils have exited special education.[30]

In summary, there are now five groups of pupils with disabilities with respect to achievement standards, assessments, and the use of scores in AYP determinations. These groups are summarized below in table 1.

Table 1. Categories of Pupils with Disabilities with Respect to Achievement Standards, Assessments, and AYP Determinations Under ESEA Title I-A

Type of Content Standards	Type of Achievement Standards	Type of Assessment	Cap on # of Proficient or Advanced Scores That May Be Included in AYP Determinations
Grade-level content standards	Grade-level academic achievement standards	Regular (i.e., the same as that applicable to pupils generally)	None
Grade-level content standards	Grade-level academic achievement standards	Regular with accommodations (e.g., special assistance for those with sight or hearing disabilities)	None
Grade-level content standards	Grade-level academic achievement standards	Alternate assessments based on regular, grade- level achievement standards (e.g., portfolios or performance assessments)	None
Grade-level content standards	Modified academic achievement standards	Alternate assessments based on modified academic achievement standards	In general, 2.0% of all pupils assessed
Alternate content standards	Alternate academic achievement standards	Alternate assessments based on alternate achievement standards	In general, 1.0% of all pupils assessed

Participation Rates

On March 29, 2004, ED announced that schools could meet the requirement that 95% or more of pupils (all pupils as well as pupils in each designated demographic group) participate in assessments (in order for the school or LEA to make AYP) on the basis of average participation rates for the last two or three years, rather than having to post a 95% or higher participation rate each year. In other words, if a particular demographic group of pupils in a public school has a 93% test participation rate in the most recent year, but had a 97% rate the preceding year, the 95% participation rate requirement would be met. In addition, the new guidance would allow schools to exclude pupils who fail to participate in assessments due to a "significant medical emergency" from the participation rate calculations. The new guidance further emphasizes the authority for states to allow pupils who miss a primary assessment date to take make-up tests, and to establish a minimum size for demographic groups of pupils to be considered in making AYP determinations (including those related to participation rates). According to ED, in some states, as many as 20% of the schools failing to make AYP did so on the basis of assessment participation rates alone. It is not known how many of these schools would meet the new, somewhat more relaxed standard.

LEP Pupils

In a letter dated February 19, and proposed regulations published on June 24, 2004, ED officials announced two new policies with respect to LEP pupils.[31] First, with respect to assessments, LEP pupils who have attended schools in the United States (other than Puerto Rico) for less than 10 months must participate in English language proficiency and mathematics tests. However, the participation of such pupils in reading tests (in English), as well as the inclusion of any of these pupils' test scores in AYP calculations, is to be optional (i.e., schools and LEAs need not consider the scores of first year LEP pupils in determining whether schools or LEAs meet AYP standards). Such pupils are still considered in determining whether the 95% test participation has been met.

Second, in AYP determinations, schools and LEAs may continue to include pupils in the LEP demographic category for up to two years after they have attained proficiency in English. However, these formerly LEP pupils need not be included when determining whether a school or LEA's count of LEP pupils meets the state's minimum size threshold for inclusion of the group in AYP calculations, and scores of formerly LEP pupils may not be included in state, LEA, or school report cards. Both these options, if exercised, should increase average test scores for pupils categorized as being part of the LEP group, and reduce the extent to which schools or LEAs fail to meet AYP on the basis of LEP pupil groups.

AYP Determinations for Targeted Assistance Schools

ED has released a February 4, 2004, letter to a state superintendent of education providing more flexibility in AYP determinations for targeted assistance schools.[32] Title I-A services are provided at the school level via one of two basic models: targeted assistance schools, where services are focused on individual pupils with the lowest levels of academic achievement, or schoolwide programs, in which Title I-A funds may be used to improve academic instruction for all pupils. Currently, most Title I-A programs are in targeted assistance schools, although the number of schoolwide programs has grown rapidly in recent years, and most pupils served by Title I-A are in schoolwide programs.

This policy letter gives schools and LEAs the option of considering only pupils assisted by Title I-A for purposes of making AYP determinations for individual schools. LEA and state level AYP determinations would still have to be made on the basis of all public school pupils. The impact of this authority, if utilized, is unclear. In schools using this authority, there would be an increased likelihood that pupil demographic groups would be below minimum size to be considered. At the same time, if Title I-A participants are indeed the lowest-performing pupils in targeted assistance schools, it seems unlikely that many schools would choose to base AYP determinations only on those pupils, especially given the current structure of the primary AYP requirements under NCLB (i.e., a status model, not a growth model).

Flexibility for Areas Affected by the Gulf Coast Hurricanes

Following the damage to school systems and dispersion of pupils in the wake of Hurricanes Katrina and Rita in August and September 2005, interest has been expressed by officials of states and LEAs that were damaged by the storms, and/or that enrolled pupils displaced by them, in the possibility of waiving some of NCLB's assessment, AYP, or other accountability requirements. In a series of policy letters to chief state school officers (CSSOs), the Secretary of Education has emphasized forms of flexibility already available under current law and announced a number of policy revisions and potential waivers that might be granted in the future.

In a September 29, 2005, letter to all CSSOs,[33] the Secretary of Education noted that they could exercise existing natural disaster provisions of NCLB [§1116(b)(7)(D) and (c)(10)(F)] to postpone the implementation of school or LEA improvement designations and corrective actions for schools or LEAs failing to meet AYP standards that are located in the major disaster areas in Louisiana, Alabama, Mississippi, Texas, or Florida, without a specific waiver being required. In addition, waivers of these requirements will be considered for other LEAs or schools heavily affected by enrolling large numbers of evacuee pupils. Further, all affected LEAs and schools could establish a separate subgroup for displaced students in AYP determinations based on assessments administered during the 2005-2006 school year. Pupils would appear only in the evacuee subgroup, not other demographic subgroups (e.g., economically disadvantaged or LEP). Waivers could be requested in 2006 to allow schools or LEAs to meet AYP requirements if only the test scores of the evacuee subgroup would prevent them from making AYP. In any case, all such students must still be assessed and the assessment results reported to the public.[34]

State Revisions of Their Accountability Plans

Over the period following the initial submission and approval of state accountability plans for AYP and related policies in 2003 through the present, many states have proposed a number of revisions to their plans. Sometimes these revisions seem clearly intended to take advantage of new forms of flexibility announced by ED officials, such as those discussed above, while in other cases states appear to be attempting to take advantage of options or forms of flexibility that reportedly been approved for other states previously.

The proposed changes in state accountability plans have apparently almost always been in the direction of increased flexibility for states and LEAs, with reductions anticipated in the number or percentage of schools or LEAs identified as failing to make AYP. Issues that have arisen with respect to these changes include a lack of transparency, and possibly inconsistencies (especially over time), in the types of changes that ED officials have approved; debates over whether the net effect of the changes is to make the accountability requirements more reasonable or to undesirably weaken them; concern that the changes may make an already complicated accountability system even more complex; and timing — whether decisions on proposed changes are being made in a timely manner by ED.

The major aspects of state accountability plans for which changes have been proposed and approved include the following: (a) changes to take advantage of revised federal regulations and policy guidance regarding assessment of pupils with the most significant cognitive disabilities, LEP pupils, and test participation rates; (b) limiting identification for improvement to schools that fail to meet AYP in the same subject area for two or more consecutive years, and limiting identification of LEAs for improvement to those that failed to meet AYP in the same subject area and across all three grade spans for two or more consecutive years; (c) using alternative methods to determine AYP for schools with very low enrollment; (d) initiating or expanding use of confidence intervals in AYP determinations, including "safe harbor" calculations; (e) changing (usually effectively increasing) minimum group size; and (f) changing graduation rate targets for high schools. Accountability plan changes that have frequently been requested but not approved by ED include (a) identification of schools for improvement only if they failed to meet AYP with respect to the same pupil group *and* subject area for two or more consecutive years, and (b) retroactive application of new forms of flexibility to recalculation of AYP for previous years.[35]

Data on Schools and LEAs Identified as Failing to Meet AYP

A substantial amount of data has become available on the number of schools and LEAs that have failed to meet the AYP standards of the NCLB based on assessments administered during the 2002-2003 through 2005-2006 school years, and several states are currently releasing preliminary data based on 2006-2007 school year assessment results. A basic problem with these data is that they frequently have been incomplete and subject to change. Currently available compilations of state AYP data are discussed below in two categories: reports focusing on the number and percentage of schools failing to meet AYP standards for one or more years versus reports on the number and percentage of public schools and LEAs identified for improvement — that is, they had failed to meet AYP standards for at least two consecutive years.

Schools Failing to Meet AYP Standards for One or More Years

Beginning with the 2002-2003 school year, data on the number of schools in each state that made or did not make AYP have been reported by the states to ED, in a series of Consolidated State Performance Reports. Until recently, these Reports were not disseminated by ED; however, the Consolidated State Performance Reports for the 2004-2005 and 2005-2006 school years have recently been made available by ED.[36]

According to these Consolidated State Performance Reports,[37] for the nation overall, 28% of all public schools failed to make adequate yearly progress based on assessment scores for the 2005-2006 school year. The percentage of public schools failing to make adequate yearly progress for 2005-2006 varied widely among the states, from 4% for Wisconsin and 9% for Louisiana to 86% for the District of Columbia and 71% for Florida. Table 2 provides the percentage of schools failing to make adequately yearly progress, based on 2005-2006 assessment results, for each state.

Schools Failing to Meet AYP Standards for Two Consecutive Years or More

A compilation of data on schools identified for improvement was published by *Education Daily[38]* in February 2006. According to this survey, 11,524 schools, or 13% of all public schools, were identified as needing improvement based on assessment results for the 2004-2005 and preceding school years. In several states, this group included at least some non-Title I schools. With respect to the various stages of school improvement, a total of 3,757 schools had failed to meet AYP standards for two consecutive years (only), 3,696 for a third year, 1,254 for a fourth year, and 1,847 for a fifth year or beyond. More recently, preliminary AYP results based on spring 2006 testing, published by *Education Week*,[39] indicate that for 34 states plus the District of Columbia, the percentage of public schools identified for improvement rose somewhat, from 13% based on spring 2005 testing to 17% based on spring 2006 results.

ED, in its "National Assessment of Title I: Interim Report," published in February 2006, reported that 13% of all public schools were identified for improvement based on assessment results through the 2003-2004 school year. This included 9,028 Title I-A schools, or 18% of all Title I-A schools. Schools most likely to be identified were those in large, urban LEAs, schools with high pupil poverty rates, and middle schools.

LEAs Failing to Meet AYP Standards

Although most attention, in both the statute and implementation activities, thus far has been focused on application of the AYP concept to schools, a limited amount of information is becoming available about LEAs that fail to meet AYP requirements, and the consequences for them. According to the Consolidated State Performance Reports referred to above, approximately 30% of all LEAs failed to meet AYP standards on the basis of assessment results for the 2005-2006 school year (see table 2).[40] Among the states, there was even greater variation for LEAs than for schools. Two states — Alabama[41] and Michigan — reported that none of their LEAs failed to make adequate yearly progress, and Wisconsin reported that only 1 of the state's 426 LEAs failed to make AYP, while 100% of the LEAs in Florida and South Carolina, plus the single, statewide LEA in Hawaii, failed to meet AYP standards.

A large number of states have recently adopted policies under which LEAs would be identified as needing improvement only if they failed to make AYP in the same subject (reading or mathematics) in each of three grade levels (elementary, middle, and high) for two or more consecutive school years. According to a recent study of NCLB implementation in six states by the Harvard Civil Rights Project, this has substantially increased the proportion of LEAs identified for improvement that serve central city areas and racially diverse and/or high poverty pupil populations.[42]

Table 2. Reported Percentage of Public Schools and Local Educational Agencies (LEAs) Failing to Make Adequate Yearly Progress (AYP) Based on Spring 2006 Assessment Results

State	Reported Percentage of Rated Schools Not Making AYP, 2006	Reported Percentage of LEAs Not Making AYP, 2006
Alabama	11	0%
Alaska	38	54
Arizona	33	39
Arkansas	39	2
California	34	37
Colorado	25	40
Connecticut	34	19
Delaware	19	11
District of Columbia	86	94
Florida	71	100
Georgia	21	65
Hawaii	65	100
Idaho	27	48
Illinois	21	23
Indiana	51	27
Iowa	17	4
Kansas	14	12
Kentucky	34	56
Louisiana	9	39
Maine[b]	19	NA[c]
Maryland	23	13
Massachusetts	41	64
Michigan	14	0
Minnesota	31	46
Mississippi	16	48
Missouri	29	39
Montana	10	16
Nebraska	18	29
Nevada	47	12
New Hampshire	39	32
New Jersey	29	13
New Mexico	54	76
New York	29	45
North Carolina	56	97
North Dakota	10	11
Ohio	39	68
Oklahoma	11	19
Oregon	32	63
Pennsylvania	18	5
Rhode Island	32	39
South Carolina	62	100
South Dakota	20	4
Tennessee	17	7
Texas	19	13
Utah	12	15
Vermont	25	26
Virginia	23	37
Washington	16	25
West Virginia	14	91

Table 2. (Continued).

State	Reported Percentage of Rated Schools Not Making AYP, 2006	Reported Percentage of LEAs Not Making AYP, 2006
Wisconsin	4	0%
Wyoming	15	10
National Average	28	30

Source: State Consolidated Performance Reports [http://www.ed.gov/admins/lead/account/consolidated/sy05-06/index.html] for all states except Maine.

a. While Alabama reports that all of its LEAs made AYP based on assessment scores for the 2005-2006 school year, it also lists 43 LEAs, or 33% of the state total number of LEAs, as being in improvement status for the 2006-2007 school year. b. For Maine, the data for schools were acquired from the state educational agency [http://www.maine.gov/education/pressreleases/ayp/ayplistmenu.htm]. c. NA = Not available. Thus, the national total for LEAs excludes Maine. d. While Michigan reports that all of its LEAs made AYP based on assessment scores for the 2005-2006 school year, it also lists 11 LEAs, or 2% of the state total number of LEAs, as being in improvement status for the 2006-2007 school year. e. Wisconsin reports one LEA as failing to make AYP out of a total of 426 LEAs.

Issues in State Implementation of NCLB Provisions

Introduction

The primary challenge associated with the AYP concept is to develop and implement school, LEA, and state performance measures that are: (a) challenging, (b) provide meaningful incentives to work toward continuous improvement, (c) are at least minimally consistent across LEAs and states, and (d) focus attention especially on disadvantaged pupil groups. At the same time, it is generally deemed desirable that AYP standards should allow flexibility to accommodate myriad variations in state and local conditions, demographics, and policies, and avoid the identification of so many schools and LEAs as failing to meet the standards that morale declines significantly systemwide and it becomes extremely difficult to target technical assistance and corrective actions on low-performing schools. The AYP provisions of NCLB are challenging and complex, and have generated substantial criticism from several states, LEAs, and interest groups. Many critics are especially concerned that efforts to direct resources and apply corrective actions to low-performing schools would likely be ineffective if resources and attention are dispersed among a relatively large proportion of public schools. Others defend NCLB's requirements as being a measured response to the weaknesses of the pre-NCLB AYP provisions, which were much more flexible but, as discussed above, had several weaknesses.

The remainder of this report provides a discussion and analysis of several specific aspects of NCLB's AYP provisions that have attracted significant attention and debate. These include the provision for an ultimate goal, use of confidence intervals and data-averaging, population diversity effects, minimum pupil group size (n), separate focus on specific pupil groups, number of schools identified and state variations therein, the 95% participation rule, state variations in assessments and proficiency standards, and timing.

It should be noted that this report focuses on issues that have arisen in the implementation of NCLB provisions on AYP. As such, it generally does not focus on alternatives to the current statutory provisions of NCLB.

Ultimate Goal

The required incorporation of an ultimate goal — of all pupils at a proficient or higher level of achievement within 12 years of enactment — is one of the most significant differences between the AYP provisions of NCLB and those under previous legislation. Setting such a date is perhaps the primary mechanism requiring state AYP standards to incorporate annual increases in expected achievement levels, as opposed to the relatively static expectations embodied in most state AYP standards under the previous IASA. Without an ultimate goal of having all pupils reach the proficient level of achievement by a specific date, states might simply establish relative goals (e.g., performance must be as high as the state average) that provide no real movement toward, or incentives for, significant improvement, especially among disadvantaged pupil groups.

Nevertheless, a goal of having all pupils at a proficient or higher level of achievement, within 12 years or any other specified period of time, may be easily criticized as being "unrealistic," if one assumes that "proficiency" has been established at a challenging level. Proponents of such a demanding ultimate goal argue that schools and LEAs frequently meet the goals established for them, even rather challenging goals, if the goals are very clearly identified, defined, and established, if they are attainable, and if it is made visibly clear that they will be expected to meet them. This is in contrast to a pre-NCLB system under which performance goals were often vague, undemanding, and poorly communicated, with few, if any, consequences for failing to meet them. A demanding goal might maximize efforts toward improvement by state public school systems, even if the goal is not met. Further, if a less ambitious goal were to be adopted, what lower level of pupil performance might be acceptable, and for which pupils?

At the same time, by setting deadlines by which all pupils must achieve at the proficient or higher level, the AYP provisions of NCLB create an incentive for states to weaken their pupil performance standards to make them easier to meet. In many states, only a minority of pupils (sometimes a small minority) are currently achieving at the proficient or higher level on state reading and mathematics assessments. Even in states where the percentage of all pupils scoring at the proficient or higher level is substantially higher, the percentage of those in many of the pupil groups identified under NCLB's AYP provisions is substantially lower. It would be extremely difficult for such states to reach a goal of 100% of their pupils at the proficient level, even within 10-12 years, without reducing their performance standards.

There has thus far been some apparent movement toward lowering proficiency standards in a small number of states. Reportedly, a few states have redesignated lower standards (e.g., "basic" or "partially proficient") as constituting a "proficient" level of performance for Title I-A purposes, or established new "proficient" levels of performance that are below levels previously understood to constitute that level of performance, and other states have considered such actions.[43] For example, in submitting its accountability plan (which was approved by ED), Colorado stated that it would deem students performing at both its "proficient" and "partially proficient" levels, as defined by that state, as being "proficient" for

NCLB purposes.[44] In its submission, the state argued that "Colorado's standards for all students remain high in comparison to most states. Colorado's basic proficiency level on CSAP is also high in comparison to most states." Similarly, Louisiana decided to identify its "basic" level of achievement as the "proficient" level for NCLB purposes, stating that "[t]hese standards have been shown to be high; for example, equipercentile equating of the standards has shown that Louisiana's 'Basic' is somewhat more rigorous than NAEP's 'Basic.' In addition, representatives from Louisiana's business community and higher education have validated the use of 'Basic' as the state's proficiency goal."[45]

This is an aspect of NCLB's AYP provisions on which there will likely be continuing debate and, possibly, future adjustments. It is unlikely that any state, and few schools or LEAs of substantial size and a heterogeneous pupil population, will meet NCLB's ultimate AYP goal, unless state standards of proficient performance are significantly lowered and/or states aggressively pursue the use of such statistical techniques as setting high minimum group sizes and confidence intervals (described below) to substantially reduce the range of pupil groups considered in AYP determinations and/or effectively lower required achievement level thresholds.

Some states have addressed this situation, at least in the short run, by "backloading" their AYP standards, requiring much more rapid improvements in performance at the end of the 12-year period than at the beginning. These states have followed the letter of the statutory language that requires increases of "equal increments" in levels of performance after the first two years, and at least once every three years thereafter.[46] However, they have "backloaded" this process by, for example, requiring increases only once every two-three years at the beginning, then requiring increases of the same degree every year for the final years of the period leading up to 2013-2014. For example, both Indiana and Ohio established incremental increases in the threshold level of performance for schools and LEAs that are equal in size, and that are to take effect in the school years beginning in 2004, 2007, 2010, 2111, 2012, and 2013. As a result, the required increases per year are three times greater during 2010-2013 than in the 2004-2009 period. These states may be trying to postpone required increases in performance levels until NCLB provisions are reconsidered, and possibly revised, by Congress.

Confidence Intervals and Data-Averaging

Many states have used one or both of a pair of statistical techniques to attempt to improve the validity and reliability of AYP determinations. Use of these techniques also tends to have an effect, whether intentional or not, of reducing the number of schools or LEAs identified as failing to meet AYP standards.

The averaging of test score results for various pupil groups over two- or three-year periods is explicitly authorized under NCLB, and this authority is used by many states. In some cases, schools or LEAs are allowed to select whether to average test score data, and for what period (two years or three), whichever is most favorable for them. As discussed above, recent policy guidance also explicitly allows the use of averaging for participation rates.

The use of another statistical technique was not explicitly envisioned in the drafting of NCLB's AYP provisions, but its inclusion in the accountability plans of several states has been approved by ED. This is the use of "confidence intervals," usually with respect to test scores, but in a couple of states also to the determination of minimum group size (see below). This concept is based on the assumption that any test administration represents a "sample survey" of pupils' educational achievement level. As with all sample surveys, there is a degree of uncertainty regarding how well the sample results — average test scores for the pupil group —reflect pupils' actual level of achievement. As with surveys, the larger the number of pupils in the group being tested, the greater the probability that the group's average test score will represent their true level of achievement, all else being equal. Put another way, confidence intervals are used to evaluate whether achievement scores are below the required threshold to a statistically significant extent.

"Confidence intervals" may be seen as "windows" surrounding a threshold test score level (i.e., the percentage of pupils at the proficient or higher level required under the state's AYP standards).[47] The size of the window varies with respect to the number of pupils in the relevant group who are tested, and with the desired degree of probability that the group's average score represents their true level of achievement. This is analogous to the "margin of error" commonly reported along with opinion polls. While test results are not based on a small sample of the relevant population, as are opinion poll results, since the tests are to be administered to the full "universe" of pupils, the results from any particular test administration are considered to be only estimates of pupils' true level of achievement, or of the effectiveness of a school or LEA in educating specified pupil groups, and thus the "margin of error" or "confidence interval" concepts are deemed by many to be relevant to these test scores. The probability, or level of confidence, is most often set at 95%, but in some cases may be as low as 90% or as high as 99% — that is, it is 95% (or 90% or 99%) certain that the true achievement level for a group of pupils is within the relevant confidence interval of test scores above and below the average score for the group. All other relevant factors being equal, the smaller the pupil group, and the higher the desired degree of probability, the larger is the window surrounding the threshold percentage.

For example, consider a situation where the threshold percentage of pupils at the proficient or higher level of achievement in reading for elementary schools required under a state's AYP standards is 40%. Without applying confidence intervals, a school would simply fail to make AYP if the average scores of all of its pupils, or of any of its relevant pupil groups meeting minimum size thresholds, is below 40%. In contrast, if confidence intervals are applied, windows are established above and below the 40% threshold, turning the threshold from a single point to a variable range of scores. The size of this score range or window will vary depending on the size of the pupil group whose average scores are being considered, and the desired degree of probability (95% or 99%) that the average achievement levels for pupils in each group are being correctly categorized as being "truly" below the required threshold. In this case, a school would fail to make AYP with respect to a pupil group only if the average score for the group is below the lowest score in that range.[48]

The use of confidence intervals to determine whether group test scores fall below required thresholds to a statistically significant degree improves the validity of AYP determinations, and addresses the fact that test scores for any group of pupils will vary from one test administration to another, and these variations may be especially large for a relatively small group of pupils. At the same time, the use of confidence intervals reduces the likelihood that schools or (to a lesser extent) LEAs will be identified as failing to make AYP. Also, for relatively small pupil groups and high levels of desired accuracy (especially a 99% probability), the size of confidence intervals may be relatively large. Ultimately, the use of this technique may mean that the average achievement levels of pupil groups in many schools will be well below 100% proficiency by 2013-2014, yet the schools would still meet AYP standards because the groups' scores are within the relevant confidence interval.

Population Diversity Effects

Minimum Pupil Group Size (n)

Another important technical factor in state AYP standards is the establishment of the minimum size (n) for pupil groups to be considered in AYP calculations. NCLB recognizes that in the disaggregation of pupil data for schools and LEAs, there might be pupil groups that are so small that average test scores would not be statistically reliable, or the dissemination of average scores for the group might risk violation of pupils' privacy rights.

Both the statute and ED regulations and other policy guidance have left the selection of this minimum number to state discretion. While most states have reportedly selected a minimum group size between 30 and 50 pupils, the range of selected values for "n" is rather large, varying from as few as five to as many as 200 pupils[49] under certain circumstances. One state (North Dakota) has set no specific level for "n," relying only on the use of confidence intervals (see above) to establish reliability of test results. While most states have always set a standard minimum size for all pupil groups, some states until recently established higher levels of "n" for pupils with disabilities and/or LEP pupils.[50]

In general, the higher the minimum group size, the less likely that many pupil groups will actually be separately considered in AYP determinations. (Pupils will still be considered, but only as part of the "all pupils" group, or possibly other specified groups.) This gives schools and LEAs fewer thresholds to meet, and reduces the likelihood that they will be found to have failed to meet AYP standards. In many cases, if a pupil group falls below the minimum group size at the school level, it is still considered at the LEA level (where it is more likely to meet the threshold). In addition, since minimum group sizes for reporting achievement data are typically lower than those used for AYP purposes,[51] scores are often reported for pupil groups who are not separately considered in AYP calculations. At the same time, relatively high levels for "n" weaken NCLB's specific focus on a variety of pupil groups, many of them disadvantaged, such as LEP pupils, pupils with disabilities, or economically disadvantaged pupils.

Separate Focus on Specific Pupil Groups

There are several ongoing issues regarding NCLB's requirement for disaggregation of pupil achievement results in AYP standards, namely the requirement that a variety of pupil groups be separately considered in AYP calculations. The first of these was discussed immediately above: the establishment of minimum group size, with the possible result that relatively small pupil groups will not be considered in the schools and LEAs of states that set "n" at a comparatively high level, especially in states that set a higher level for certain groups (e.g., pupils with disabilities) than others.

A second issue arises from the fact that the definition of the specified pupil groups has been left essentially to state discretion. This is noteworthy particularly with respect to two groups of pupils: LEP pupils and pupils in major racial and ethnic groups. Regarding LEP pupils, many have been concerned about the difficulty of demonstrating that these pupils are performing at a proficient level if this pupil group is defined narrowly to include only pupils unable to perform in regular English-language classroom settings. In other words, if pupils who no longer need special language services are no longer identified as being LEP, how will it be possible to bring those who are identified as LEP up to a proficient level of achievement?

In developing their AYP standards, some states addressed this concern by including pupils in the LEP category for one or more years after they no longer need special language services. As was discussed above, ED has recently published policy guidance encouraging all states to follow this approach, allowing them to continue to include pupils in the LEP group for up to two years after being mainstreamed into regular English language instruction, and further allowing the scores of LEP pupils to be excluded from AYP calculations for the first year of pupils' enrollment in United States schools. If widely adopted, these policies should reduce the extent that schools or LEAs are identified as failing to meet AYP standards on the basis of the LEP pupil group.

Another aspect of this issue arises from the discretion given to states in defining "major racial and ethnic groups." Neither the statute nor ED has defined this term. Some states defined the term relatively comprehensively (e.g., Maryland includes American Indian, African American, Asian, White, and Hispanic pupil groups) and some more narrowly (e.g., Texas identifies only three groups — White, African American, and Hispanic). A more narrow interpretation may reduce the attention focused on excluded pupil groups. It would also reduce the number of different thresholds some schools and LEAs would have to meet in order to make AYP.

A final, overarching issue arises from the relationship between pupil diversity in schools and LEAs and the likelihood of being identified as failing to meet AYP standards. All other relevant factors being equal (especially the minimum group size criteria), the more diverse the pupil population, the more thresholds a school or LEA must meet in order to make AYP. While in a sense this was an intended result of legislation designed to focus (within limits) on all pupil groups, the impact of making it more difficult for schools and LEAs serving diverse populations to meet AYP standards may also be seen as an unintended consequence of NCLB. This issue has been analyzed in a recent study by Thomas J. Kane and Douglas O. Staiger, who concluded that such "subgroup targets cause large numbers of schools to fail ... arbitrarily single out schools with large minority subgroups for sanctions ... or statistically disadvantage diverse schools that are likely to be attended by minority students.... Moreover, while the costs of the subgroup targets are clear, the benefits are not. Although these targets are meant to encourage schools to focus more on the achievement of minority youth, we find no association between the application of subgroup targets and test score performance among minority youth."[52] Thus far, insufficient data are available to evaluate whether this prediction is being borne out in practice.

An additional study published by Policy Analysis for California Education (PACE)[53] found that when comparing public schools in California with similar aggregate pupil achievement levels, schools with larger numbers of different NCLB-relevant demographic groups were substantially less likely to have met AYP standards in the 2002-2003 school year. Similarly when comparing California public schools with comparable percentages of pupils from low-income families, schools with larger numbers of relevant demographic groups of pupils were much less likely to have met AYP.

However, without specific requirements for achievement gains by each of the major pupil groups, it is possible that insufficient attention would be paid to the performance of the disadvantaged pupil groups among whom improvements are most needed, and for whose benefit the Title I-A program was established. Under previous law, without an explicit, specific requirement that AYP standards focus on these disadvantaged pupil groups, most state AYP definitions considered only the performance of all pupils combined. And it is theoretically possible for many schools and LEAs to demonstrate substantial improvements in achievement by their pupils overall while the achievement of their disadvantaged pupils does not improve significantly, at least until the ultimate goal of all pupils at the proficient or higher level of achievement is approached. This is especially true under a "status" model of AYP such as the one in NCLB, under which advantaged pupil groups may have achievement levels well above what is required, and an overall achievement level could easily mask achievement well below the required threshold by various groups of disadvantaged pupils.

One possible alternative to current policy would be to allow states to count each student only once, in net, in AYP calculations, with equal fractions for each relevant demographic category (e.g., a Hispanic LEP pupil from a low-income family would count as one-third of a pupil in each group).

NUMBER OF SCHOOLS IDENTIFIED AND STATE VARIATIONS THEREIN

As was discussed earlier, concern has been expressed by some analysts since early debates on NCLB that a relatively high proportion of schools would fail to meet AYP standards. On the basis of assessment results for 2004-2005, approximately 26% of all public schools nationwide failed to make AYP, and approximately 14% of all public schools were identified as needing improvement (i.e., failed to meet AYP standards for two or more consecutive years). Future increases in performance thresholds, as the ultimate goal of all pupils at the proficient or higher level of achievement is approached, as well as implementation of tests in additional grades in many states,[54] may result in higher percentages of schools failing to make AYP.

In response to these concerns, ED officials have emphasized the importance of taking action to identify and move to improve underperforming schools, no matter how numerous. They have also emphasized the possibilities for flexibility and variation in taking corrective actions with respect to schools that fail to meet AYP, depending on the extent to which they fail to meet those standards. It should also be re-emphasized that many of the schools reported as having failed to meet AYP standards have failed to meet AYP for one year only, while NCLB requires that a series of actions be taken only with respect to schools or LEAs participating in ESEA Title I-A that fail to meet AYP for two consecutive years or more.

Further, some analysts argue that a set of AYP standards that one-quarter or more of public schools fail to meet may accurately reflect pervasive weaknesses in public school systems, especially with respect to the performance of disadvantaged pupil groups. To these analysts, the identification of large percentages of schools is a positive sign of the rigor and challenge embodied in NCLB's AYP requirements, and is likely to provide needed motivation for significant improvement (and ultimately a reduction in the percentage of schools so identified).

Others have consistently expressed concern about the accuracy and efficacy of an accountability system under which such a high percentage of schools is identified as failing to make adequate progress, with consequent strain on financial and other resources necessary to provide technical assistance, public school choice and supplemental services options, as well as other corrective actions. In addition, some have expressed concern that schools might be more likely to fail to meet AYP simply because they have diverse enrollments, and therefore more groups of pupils to be separately considered in determining whether the school meets AYP standards. They also argue that the application of technical assistance and, ultimately, corrective actions to such a high percentage of schools will dilute available resources to such a degree that these responses to inadequate performance would be insufficient to markedly improve performance. A few analysts even speculate that the AYP system under NCLB is intended to portray large segments of American public education as having "failed," leading to proposals for large scale privatization of elementary and secondary education.[55]

The proportion of public schools identified as failing to meet AYP standards is not only relatively large in the aggregate, but also varies widely among the states. As was discussed above, the percentage of public schools identified as failing to make AYP on the basis of assessment results for 2004-2005 ranged from 2% to approximately two-thirds for the states for which data are available. This result is somewhat ironic, given that one of the major criticisms of the pre-NCLB provisions for AYP was that they resulted in a similarly wide degree of state variation in the proportion of schools identified, and the more consistent structure required under NCLB was widely expected to lead to at least somewhat greater consistency among states in the proportion of schools identified.

It seems likely that the pre-NCLB variations in the proportion of schools failing to meet AYP reflected large differences in the nature and structure of state AYP standards, as well as major differences in the nature and rigor of state pupil performance standards and assessments. While the basic structure of AYP definitions is now substantially more consistent across states, significant variations remain with respect to the factors discussed in this section of the report (such as minimum group size), and substantial differences in the degree of challenge embodied in state standards and assessments remain. Overall, it seems likely that the key influences determining the percentage of a state's schools that fails to make AYP include (in no particular order): (1) degree of rigor in state content and pupil performance standards; (2) minimum pupil group size (n) in AYP determinations; (3) use of confidence intervals in AYP determinations (and whether at a 95% or 99% level of confidence); (4) extent of diversity in pupil population; (5) extent of communication about, and understanding of, the 95% test participation rule, and (6) possible actual differences in educational quality.

95% Participation Rule

It appears that in many cases, schools or LEAs have failed to meet AYP solely because of low participation rates in assessments, meaning that fewer than 95% of all pupils, or of pupils in relevant demographic groups meeting the minimum size threshold, took the assessments. While, as discussed above, ED recently published policy guidance that relaxes the participation rate requirement somewhat — allowing use of average rates over two- to three-year periods, and excusing certain pupils for medical reasons — the high rate of assessment participation that is required in order for schools or LEAs to meet AYP standards is likely to remain an ongoing focus of debate.

Although few argue against having any participation rate requirement, it may be questioned whether it needs to be as high as 95%. In recent years, the overall percentage of enrolled pupils who attend public schools each day has been approximately 93.5%, and it is generally agreed that attendance rates are lower in schools serving relatively high proportions of disadvantaged pupils. Even though schools are explicitly allowed to administer assessments on make-up days following the primary date of test administration, and it is probable that more schools and LEAs will meet this requirement as they become more fully aware of its significance, it is likely to continue to be very difficult for many schools and LEAs to meet a 95% test participation requirement.

State Variations in Assessments and Proficiency Standards

As noted above, it is likely that state variations in the percentage of schools failing to meet AYP standards are based not only on underlying differences in achievement levels, as well as a variety of technical factors in state AYP provisions, but also on differences in the degree of rigor or challenge in state pupil performance standards and assessments. Particularly now that all states receiving Title I-A grants must also participate in state-level administration of NAEP tests in 4th and 8th grade reading and math every two years, this variation can be illustrated for all states by comparing the percentage of pupils scoring at the proficient level on NAEP versus state assessments.

Such a comparison was conducted by a private organization, Achieve, Inc., based on 8th grade reading and math assessments administered in the spring of 2003.[56] For a variety of reasons (e.g., several states did not administer standards-based assessments in reading or math to 8th grade pupils in 2003), the analysis excluded several states; 29 states were included in the comparison for reading, and 32 states for math. According to this analysis, the percentage of pupils statewide who score at a proficient or higher level on state assessments, using state-specific pupil performance standards, was generally much higher than the percentage deemed to be at the proficient or higher level on the NAEP tests, and employing NAEP's pupil performance standards. Of the states considered, the percentage of pupils scoring at a proficient or higher level on the state assessment was lower than on NAEP (implying a more rigorous state standard) for five states[57] (out of 32) in math and only two states (out of 29) in reading. Further, among the majority of states where the percentage of pupils at the proficient level or above was found to be higher on state assessments than on NAEP, the relationship between the size of the two groups varied widely — in some cases only marginally higher on the state assessment, and in others the percentage at the proficient level was more than twice as high on the state assessment as on NAEP. While some portion of these differences in performance may result from differences in the motivation of pupils to perform well (and of teachers to encourage high performance) on NAEP versus state assessments, comparisons to NAEP results help to illuminate the variations in state proficiency standards. It is not yet clear whether such comparisons will significantly encourage greater consistency in those standards.

A second issue is whether some states might choose to lower their standards of "proficient" performance, in order to reduce the number of schools identified as failing to meet AYP and make it easier to meet the ultimate NCLB goal of all pupils at the proficient or higher level within 12 years. In the affected states, this would increase the percentage of pupils deemed to be achieving at a "proficient" level, and reduce the number of schools failing to meet AYP standards.

Although states are generally free to take such actions without jeopardizing their eligibility for Title I-A grants, because performance standards are ultimately state-determined and have always varied significantly, such actions have elicited public criticism from ED. In a policy letter dated October 22, 2002, the Secretary of Education stated

> Unfortunately, some states have lowered the bar of expectations to hide the low performance of their schools. And a few others are discussing how they can ratchet down their standards in order to remove schools from their lists of low performers. Sadly, a small number of persons have suggested reducing standards for defining "proficiency" in order to artificially present the facts.... Those who play semantic games or try to tinker with state numbers to lock out parents and the public, stand in the way of progress and reform. They are the enemies of equal justice and equal opportunity. They are apologists for failure.[58]

REFERENCES

[1] These corrective actions, as well as possible performance-based awards, are not discussed in detail in this report. For information on them, see CRS Report RL31487, *Education for the Disadvantaged: Overview of ESEA Title I-A Amendments Under the No Child Left Behind Act*, by Wayne Riddle.

[2] For additional information on this legislation, see CRS Report 89-7, *Education for Disadvantaged Children: Major Themes in the 1988 Reauthorization of Chapter 1*, by Wayne Riddle (out of print, available from author [7-7382] upon request).

[3] For additional information on the standard and assessment requirements under ESEA title I-A, see CRS Report RL31407, *Educational Testing: Implementation of ESEA Title I-A Requirements Under the No Child Left Behind Act*, by Wayne C. Riddle.

[4] For more information on all aspects of the ESEA Title I-A assessment requirements, see CRS Report RL31407, *Educational Testing: Implementation of the ESEA Title I-A Requirements Under the No Child Left Behind Act*, by Wayne C. Riddle.

[5] All pupils in states where AYP determinations were made for all public schools, or all pupils served by ESEA Title I-A in states where AYP determinations were made only for such schools and pupils.

[6] See [http://www.cpre.org/Publications/Publications_Accountability.htm].

[7] U.S. Department of Education, Office of the Undersecretary, Policy and Program StudiesService, *Evaluation of Title I Accountability Systems and School Improvement Efforts (TASSIE): First-Year Findings*, 2004. Hereafter referred to as the TASSIE First-Year Report.

[8] See the U.S. Department of Education, "Paige Releases Number of Schools in School Improvement in Each State," press release, July 1, 2002 at [http://www.ed.gov/news/pressreleases/2002/07/07012002a.html].

[9] Another report published by ED in 2004 (the TASSIE First-Year Report — see footnote 7) stated that 8,078 public schools had been identified as failing to meet AYP standards for two or more consecutive years in the 2001-2002 school year.

[10] As is discussed later in this report and in more detail in a separate report (RL33032, *Adequate Yearly Progress (AYP): Growth Models Under the No Child Left Behind Act*), a growth model pilot project has been initiated by ED.

[11] In addition, program regulations (*Federal Register*, December 2, 2002) do not require graduation rates and other additional academic indicators to be disaggregated in determining whether schools or LEAs meet AYP standards.

[12] States may, of course, establish starting points above the required level.

[13] The "base year" is the 2001-2002 school year.

[14] This is determined by ranking all public schools (of the relevant grade level) statewide according to their percentage of pupils at the proficient or higher level of achievement (based on all pupils in each school), and setting the threshold at the point where one-fifth of the schools (weighted by enrollment) have been counted, starting with the schools at the lowest level of achievement.

[15] Under program regulations [4 C.F.R. § 200.16(c)(2)], the starting point may vary by grade span (e.g., elementary, middle, etc.) and subject.

[16] If the number of pupils in a specified demographic group is too small to meet the minimum group size requirements for consideration in AYP determinations, then the participation rate requirement does not apply.

[17] The plans have been posted online by ED at [http://www.ed.gov/admins/lead/account/stateplans03/index.html].

[18] See [http://www.ed.gov/news/pressreleases/2002/07/07242002.html].

[19] ED has approved state accountability plans under which schools or LEAs would be identified as failing to meet AYP only if they failed to meet the required level of performance in the same subject for two or more consecutive years, but has apparently not approved proposals under which a school would be identified only if it failed to meet AYP in the same subject *and* pupil group for two or more consecutive years.

[20] See [http://www.ed.gov/news/pressreleases/2005/04/04072005.html].

[21] This topic is discussed in greater detail in the last section of this report.

[22] See "Ed Fines Texas for Missing AYP Reporting Deadline," *Education Daily*, April 26, 2005, p. 1.

[23] See [http://www.ed.gov/news/pressreleases/2005/11/11182005.html].

[24] See [http://www.ed.gov/policy/elsec/guid/growthmodelguidance.pdf].

[25] Delaware's proposal included the use of confidence intervals at an unspecified level in implementing the growth model; however, ED approved use of the model without confidence intervals.

[26] This limitation does *not* apply to the administration of alternate assessments based on the same standards applicable to all students, for other pupils with (non-cognitive or less severe cognitive) disabilities.

[27] Under current regulations, the short-term policy cannot be extended beyond the 2008-2009 school year.

[28] This would be calculated based on statewide demographic data, with the resulting percentage applied to each affected school and LEA in the state. In making the AYP determination using the adjusted data, no further use may be made of confidence intervals or other statistical techniques. (The actual, not just the adjusted, percentage of pupils who are proficient must also be reported to parents and the public.)

[29] The 3.0% limit might be exceeded for LEAs, but only if — and to the extent that — the SEA waives the 1.0% cap applicable to scores on alternate assessments based on alternate achievement standards.

[30] In such cases, the former pupils with disabilities would *not* have to be counted in determining whether the minimum group size was met for the disability subgroup.

[31] See *Federal Register*, June 24, 2004, pp. 35462-35465; and [http://www.ed.gov/nclb/accountability/schools/factsheet-english.html].

[32] See [http://www.ed.gov/policy/elsec/guid/stateletters/asaypnc.html].

[33] See [http://www.ed.gov/policy/elsec/guid/secletter/050929.html].

[34] For additional information on this topic, see CRS Report RL33236, *Education-Related Hurricane Relief: Legislative Act*, by Rebecca Skinner, *et al.*

[35] See Center on Education Policy, *Rule Changes Could Help More Schools Meet Test Score Targets for the No Child Left Behind Act*, October 22, 2004, available at [http://www.cep-dc.org/nclb/StateAccountabilityPlanAmendmentsReportOct2004.pdf]; Title I Monitor, *Changes in Accountability Plans Dilute Standards, Critics Say*, November 2004; Council of Chief State School Officers, *Revisiting Statewide Educational Accountability Under NCLB*, September 2004, available at [http://www.ccsso.org]; and "Requests Win More Leeway Under NCLB," *Education Week*, July 13, 2005, p. 1.

[36] See [http://www.ed.gov/admins/lead/account/consolidated/index.html].

[37] For one state, Maine, these data were not available in the Consolidated State Performance Report, and were obtained directly from the state educational agency.

[38] "Data analysis finds more schools subject to sanctions," *Education Daily*, February 16, 2006, pp. 1-2.

[39] See"Preliminary NCLB Results Show Slippage in 2006," *Education Week*, September 20, 2006, p. 20.

[40] This calculation was based on data for all states except Maine.

[41] See endnotes [a] and [d] in table 2 regarding the LEA data for Alabama and Michigan.

[42] Harvard Civil Rights Project, "Changing NCLB Accountability Standards: Implications for Racial Equity," June 2005, available at [http://www.civilrightsproject.harvard.edu].

[43] See, for example, "States Revise the Meaning of 'Proficient'," *Education Week*, October 9, 2002.

[44] See [http://www.ed.gov/admins/lead/account/stateplans03/cocsa.pdf], p. 7.

[45] See [http://www.ed.gov/admins/lead/account/stateplans03/lacsa.doc], p 12.

[46] According to Section 1111(b)(2)(H), "Each State shall establish intermediate goals for meeting the requirements, ... of this paragraph and that shall — (i) increase in equal increments over the period covered by the State's timeline...." The program regulations also would seem to require increases in equal increments: "Each State must establish intermediate goals that increase in equal increments over the period covered by the timeline...." (34 C.F.R. § 200.17).

[47] Alternatively, the confidence interval "window" may be applied to average test scores for each relevant pupil group, that would be compared to a fixed threshold score level to determine whether AYP has been met.

[48] The text above describes the way in which confidence intervals have been used by states for AYP determinations. The concept could be applied in a different way, requiring scores to be at or above the highest score in the "window" in order to demonstrate that a pupil group had meet AYP standards to a statistically significant degree. This would reflect confidence (at the designated level of probability) that a school or LEA had met AYP standards, whereas the current usage reflects confidence that the school or LEA had failed to meet AYP standards.

[49] In Texas, the minimum group size for pupil groups (other than the "all pupils" group, where the minimum is 40) is the greater of 50 students or 10% of all students in a school or LEA (up to a maximum of 200). In California, the minimum group size is the greater of 50 students or 15% of all students in the school or LEA (up to a maximum of 100).

[50] Under regulations published on April 9, 2007, this practice is no longer allowed.

[51] Minimum group sizes for AYP purposes are typically in the range of 30 to 40 pupils, while those for reporting are typically in the range of five to 20 pupils.

[52] Thomas J. Kane and Douglas O. Staiger, "Unintended Consequences of Racial Subgroup Rules," in Paul Peterson and Martin West, eds., *No Child Left Behind? The Politics and Practice of School Accountability* (Washington: Brookings Institution Press, 2003), pp. 152-176.

[53] John R. Novak and Bruce Fuller, *Penalizing Diverse Schools?* PACE Policy Brief 03-4, December 2003.

[54] Several states do not currently administer standards-based assessments in mathematics and reading in each of grades 3-8, or assessments in science at three grade levels, as is required in future years under NCLB. As such assessments are administered to pupils in additional grades and subject areas, there will be increases in the number of pupil groups meeting minimum size thresholds to be considered in AYP determinations, and possibly also increases in the number of different test score thresholds that many schools and LEAs have to meet.

[55] See Alfie Kohn, "Test Today, Privatize Tomorrow: Using Accountability to 'Reform' Public Schools to Death," *Phi Delta Kappan*, vol. 85, no. 8 (April 2004), pp. 568-577.

[56] Center on Education Policy, *From the Capital to the Classroom, Year 2 of the No Child Left Behind Act* (January 2004), p. 61.

[57] In two additional states, the percentages were essentially the same.

[58] See [http://www.ed.gov/news/pressreleases/2002/10/10232002a.html].

In: No Child Left Behind: Issues and Developments
Editor: P. H. Berkhart, pp. 37-53

ISBN: 978-1-60456-210-1

Chapter 2

ADEQUATE YEARLY PROGRESS (AYP): GROWTH MODELS UNDER THE NO CHILD LEFT BEHIND ACT*

Wayne C. Riddle

ABSTRACT

A key concept embodied in the accountability provisions of the Elementary and Secondary Education Act (ESEA), as amended by the No Child Left Behind Act of 2001 (NCLB, P.L. 107-110), is that of adequate yearly progress (AYP). In order to be eligible for grants under ESEA Title I, Part A — Education for Disadvantaged Pupils — states must implement AYP policies applicable to all public schools and local educational agencies (LEAs), based primarily on the scores of pupils on state assessments. Schools or LEAs that fail to meet AYP standards for two or more consecutive years face a variety of consequences.

The primary model of AYP under the NCLB is a group status model. Such models set threshold levels of performance, expressed as a percentage of pupils scoring at a proficient or higher level on state assessments of reading and mathematics, that must be met by all pupils as a group, as well as pupils in designated demographic subgroups, in order for a public school or LEA to make AYP. Current law also includes a secondary model of AYP, a "safe harbor" provision, under which a school or LEA may make AYP if, among pupil groups who did not meet the primary AYP standard, the percentage of pupils who are *not* at the proficient or higher level declines by at least 10%.

Substantial interest has been expressed in the possible use of individual/cohort growth models to meet the AYP requirements of the NCLB. Such AYP models are not consistent with certain statutory provisions of the NCLB, as those have until recently been interpreted by the U.S. Department of Education (ED). However, under a pilot program, ED has approved applications from nine states to use growth models to make AYP determinations. Many proponents of growth models of AYP see them as being more fair and accurate than the models generally employed to meet NCLB requirements, primarily because they recognize the fact that different schools and pupils have different

* Excerpted from CRS Report RL33032, dated August 2, 2007.

starting points in their achievement levels, and recognize progress being made at all levels.

Growth models of AYP have the disadvantage of implicitly setting lower initial thresholds or expectations for some pupil groups and/or schools. Although any growth model consistent with the NCLB would need to incorporate the act's ultimate goal of all pupils at a proficient or higher level of achievement by 2013-2014, such models used currently in state (non-NCLB) accountability plans do not include such goals and might allow disadvantaged schools and pupils to remain at relatively low levels of achievement for significant periods of time. Growth models of AYP may be quite complicated and may address the accountability purposes of the NCLB less directly and clearly than the currently statutory AYP models.

ESEA programs are authorized through FY2008, and it is generally assumed that the 110th Congress will actively consider legislation to amend and extend the ESEA.

A key concept embodied in the accountability provisions of the Elementary and Secondary Education Act (ESEA), as amended by the No Child Left Behind Act of 2001 (NCLB, P.L. 107-110) is that of adequate yearly progress (AYP) toward proficiency on state assessments.[1] In order to maintain eligibility for grants under ESEA Title I, Part A — Grants to Local Educational Agencies (LEAs) for the Education of Disadvantaged Pupils, the largest federal K-12 education program —states must establish and implement standards of AYP that are applicable to all public schools and LEAs in the state, as well as the state overall. These AYP standards are to be based primarily, although not solely, on the scores of all pupils as a group, as well as pupils in designated demographic subgroups, on state developed or selected assessments that are linked to state standards of curriculum content and pupil performance.[2] Schools or LEAs that fail to meet AYP standards for two or more consecutive years face a variety of consequences and, ultimately, corrective actions.[3] ESEA programs are authorized through FY2008, and it is generally assumed that the 110th Congress will actively consider legislation to amend and extend the ESEA.

Substantial interest has been expressed in the possible use of particular concepts, usually referred to as growth models, to meet the AYP requirements of the NCLB. Such AYP models are not consistent with certain statutory provisions of the NCLB, as they have until recently been interpreted by the U.S. Department of Education (ED). In November 2005, the Secretary of Education announced a growth model pilot program under which up to ten states would be allowed to use growth models to make AYP determinations for the 2005-2006 school year. The applications of nine states — North Carolina, Tennessee, Arkansas, Delaware, Florida, Iowa, Ohio, Alaska, and Arizona — have been approved to participate in the pilot program. This report discusses growth and other models for AYP determinations, and analyzes issues related to the possible use of growth models to meet the AYP requirements of the NCLB.

The Range of Possible Models for Measuring AYP for Schools and LEAs

While AYP definitions or standards may vary in a multitude of respects, their basic structure generally falls into one of three general categories. The No Child Left Behind Act statute, as implemented by ED currently, places primary emphasis on one of these models, while incorporating a second model as an explicitly authorized alternative. In recent years, critics of current policy have increasingly focused their attention on a third model of AYP, which is the primary topic of this report.

The three basic structural forms for AYP of schools or LEAs are the *group status*, *successive group improvement*, and *individual/cohort growth* models. In the context of these terms, "group" (or "subgroup," in the case of detailed demographic categories) refers to a collection of pupils that is identified by their grade level and usually other demographic characteristics (e.g., race, ethnicity, or economic disadvantage) as of a point in time, such as all Hispanic third grade pupils enrolled in a school or LEA in a particular year. The actual pupils in a "group" may change substantially, or even completely, from one year to the next. In contrast, a "cohort" refers to a collection of pupils in which the *same* pupils are followed from year-to-year, such as the Hispanic pupils who entered third grade in a school, LEA or state in fall 2002, and have been followed as a cohort since that time.

The key characteristic of the *group status* model is a fixed "annual measurable objective" (AMO), or required threshold level of achievement, that is *the same* for all pupil groups, schools, and LEAs statewide in a given subject and grade level. Under this model, performance at a point in time is compared to a benchmark at that time, with no direct consideration of changes over a previous period.

The key characteristic of the *successive group improvement* model is a focus on the *rate of change* in achievement in a subject area from one year to the next among *groups* of pupils in a grade level at a school or LEA (e.g., the percentage of this year's 5th grade pupils in a school who are at a proficient or higher level in mathematics compared to the percentage of last year's 5th grade pupils who were at a proficient or higher level of achievement).

Finally, the key characteristic of the *individual/cohort growth* model is a focus on the *rate of change* over time in the level of achievement among *cohorts* of the same pupils. Such models may compare current performance of specific pupils or cohorts to past performance, or may project future performance of pupils/cohorts based on past changes in their performance level. Growth models are *longitudinal*, based upon the tracking of the same pupils as they progress through their K-12 education careers. While the progress of pupils is tracked individually, results are typically aggregated when used for accountability purposes. Aggregation may be by demographic group, by school or LEA, or other relevant characteristics. In general, growth models would give credit for meeting steps along the way to proficiency in ways that a status model typically does not.[4]

To help illustrate the basic differences among these three AYP models, simplified examples of basic aspects of each are described below. The reader should keep in mind many other variations of these model types are possible.

- A *group status* model, such as the current primary model of AYP under the NCLB (described further below), establishes a series of threshold levels or AMOs, which are percentages of pupils scoring at a proficient or higher level of achievement on state standards-based assessments of reading and mathematics. These AMOs have a starting point and a series of increases toward (in the case of the NCLB) an ultimate goal of 100% of pupils at a proficient or higher level of achievement, covering a multi-year period (for the NCLB, the period of 2001-2002 through 2013-2014). These AMOs are specific to each grade level and subject (reading or mathematics) at which state assessments are administered. A key feature of the AMOs in this model is that they are the same for all pupil groups —the "all pupil" group as well as each of the demographic subgroups specified under the NCLB (pupils with disabilities, pupils from low-income families, pupils with limited English proficiency, etc.). This model focuses solely on current year performance of the pupils currently enrolled in each school/LEA for every grade level at which assessments are administered.[5] Comparisons to previous year performance play no role in AYP determinations.

- An example of a simplified *successive group improvement* model is the secondary ("safe harbor") model authorized under the NCLB. Under this model, as embodied in the NCLB, the basic structure of the AYP system is the same as described above, but the primary focus shifts to the change from the previous year for each group assessed. If any specified demographic group fails to meet the primary group status AYP criterion described above, the school or LEA is still deemed to meet AYP standards if the percentage of pupils scoring *below* the proficient level declines by 10% in comparison to the previous year for pupils in that grade level and demographic group. Thus, the primary focus shifts to the *change* in achievement from the previous year, comparing (for example) this year's pupils from low-income families in the particular school/LEA/grade level to last year's pupils from low-income families enrolled in that school/LEA/grade level (i.e., the pupils are in the same demographic category, but are not necessarily the same pupils).[6]
- An *individual/cohort growth* model begins by tracking the performance of individual pupils over multiple (at least two) years. The performance of pupils in the same grade level who share relevant demographic characteristics within a school, LEA, or the state overall may be combined into a cohort. The *change* in scores for this cohort is compared to a standard of *expected growth*. The expected growth may be either "data-driven" (e.g., the statewide average rate of achievement growth for all pupils, or the predicted rate of growth statewide for pupils with similar demographic characteristics), or "policy-driven" (a multi-year growth path sufficient to meet an ultimate goal, such as the NCLB requirement for all pupils to reach a proficient or higher level of achievement by 2013-2014). A school or LEA is deemed to meet AYP requirements if the achievement growth of each relevant cohort of pupils meets the expected level of growth. The path of expected growth, as well as the starting points for the growth path, will likely differ for each relevant demographic group of pupils.

Some growth models also incorporate a variety of statistical controls, adjustments to account for pupil demographic characteristics or past achievement, to sharpen the focus on estimating the impact of specific teachers, schools, or LEAs on pupil achievement and to measure pupil growth against *predicted* growth for pupils with similar characteristics, but these are not essential elements of all growth models. Proponents argue that such models, with their controls for background characteristics and past learning, maximize the focus on factors that are under the control of teachers and other school staff. The Tennessee Value-Added Assessment System (TVAAS) is one specific form of growth model that uses pupil background characteristics, previous performance, and other data as statistical controls in order to focus on estimating the specific effects of particular schools, districts, teachers or programs on pupil achievement.[7]

THE AYP MODELS EXPLICITLY AUTHORIZED BY THE NCLB

The primary model of AYP under the NCLB currently is a group status model. As noted in the example above, group status models set as their AMOs threshold levels of performance, expressed specifically in terms of the percentage of pupils scoring at a proficient or higher (advanced) level on state assessments of reading and mathematics. These AMOs must be met by any school or LEA, both overall and with respect to all relevant pupil subgroups, in order to make AYP, whatever the school's or LEA's "starting point" (for the multi-year period covered by the accountability policy) or performance in the previous year. This AMO "uniform bar" is applicable to all pupil subgroups of sufficient size to be considered in AYP determinations. The threshold levels of achievement are to be set separately for reading and math, and may be set separately for each level of K-12 education (elementary, middle, and high schools). For example, it might be required that 45% or more of the pupils in any of a state's public elementary schools score at the proficient or higher level of achievement in reading in order for a school to make AYP.[8]

The initial minimum starting point for the "uniform bar" is to be the greater of (a) the percentage of pupils at the proficient or advanced level of achievement for the lowest-achieving pupil subgroup in the base year (2001-2002), or (b) the percentage of pupils at the proficient or advanced level of achievement for the lowest-performing quintile (5th)[9] of schools statewide in the base year.[10] The "uniform bar" must generally be raised at least once every three years, although in the initial period it must be increased after no more than two years. Such group status models attempt to emphasize the importance of meeting certain minimum levels of achievement for all pupil groups, schools, and LEAs, and arguably apply consistent expectations to all pupil groups.

The secondary model of AYP under the NCLB currently is the "safe harbor" provision, an example of a successive group improvement model.[11] This is an alternative provision under which schools or LEAs that fail to meet the usual requirements may still be deemed to have made AYP if they meet certain other conditions. A school where aggregate achievement is below the level required under the group status model described above would still be deemed to have made AYP, through the "safe harbor" provision, if, among relevant pupil groups who did not meet the primary AYP standard, the percentage of pupils who are *not* at the proficient or higher level in the school declines by at least 10% (not 10 percentage points)[12], and those pupil groups make progress on at least one other academic indicator included in the state's AYP standards.[13] For example, if the standard AMO is 45%, and a school fails to meet AYP because of the performance of one pupil group (e.g., the mathematics scores of white pupils) and the percentage of such pupils scoring at a proficient or higher level the previous year was 30%, then the school could still make AYP if the percentage of white pupils scoring at a proficient or higher level increases to at least 37% (the 30% from the previous year plus 10% of (100%-30%), or seven percentage points).

During debates over the adoption of NCLB in 2001, much of the attention was focused on successive group improvement models of AYP, not group status or individual/cohort growth models. Both the Senate-passed version, and the primary elements of the House-passed version, of the bill (H.R. 1, 107th Congress) that became NCLB embodied successive group improvement concepts of AYP.[14] Relatively little attention was paid to individual/cohort growth models during consideration of NCLB. The group status model adopted by the conferees on H.R. 1 as the primary AYP concept under NCLB substantially resembled the pre-NCLB AYP definition used in the state of Texas.

Possible reasons why relatively little attention was devoted to individual/cohort growth models of AYP during consideration of NCLB in 2001 include the fact that they were used by few states at the time to meet accountability requirements under either state law or under federal law preceding NCLB (the Improving America's Schools Act of 1994);[15] the implicit demand for resources (both extensive, pupil-level longitudinal data systems and analytical capacity in state educational agencies); their relative complexity, compared to the status and improvement models; their assumed requirement for annual pupil assessments throughout all, or at least most, of pupils' K-12 education careers, which very few states had in place; and the difficulty (although not the impossibility) of integrating into growth models an ultimate goal of all pupils at a proficient or higher level of achievement by a specified time.

The remainder of this chapter will focus almost totally on individual/cohort growth models of AYP versus group status models, and little further attention will be paid to successive group improvement models of AYP. This is primarily because the "safe harbor" alternative model of AYP is already available (unlike the individual/cohort growth model alternative), and because it has reportedly been invoked relatively infrequently. Some analysts argue the "safe harbor" provision is used infrequently because it sets a very challenging standard, at least for pupil groups that are currently at relatively low levels of proficiency,[16] and that the required 10% reduction in pupils below the proficient level should be reduced, perhaps to 3%-4%.[17]

Growth Model Alternatives to NCLB's Statutory Models of AYP

For the sake of simplicity, in the remainder of this report we will refer to the three AYP models by the abbreviated titles of "status," "improvement," and "growth" models. In recent years, as experience with NCLB requirements for AYP has been accumulated within states, LEAs, and schools, increased attention has been devoted by some analysts and administrators to the possible use of growth models of AYP under NCLB.[18] While there are many possible variations of growth models, they would all appear to violate certain explicit statutory provisions of NCLB, at least as those have been interpreted by ED separate from the growth model pilot discussed later in this report. At the least, a growth model would involve the use of differing AMOs for different cohorts of pupils, varying by pupil demographics and possibly by school or LEA as well, and this would violate the uniform bar approach of the primary AYP model of NCLB.[19] Growth models would also provide for different starting points or improvement paths for different pupils/cohorts.

Growth Model Pilot

In November 2005, the Secretary of Education announced a growth model pilot program under which up to 10 states would be allowed to use growth models to make AYP determinations for the 2005-2006 or subsequent school years.[20] The models proposed by the states must meet at least the following criteria (in addition to a variety of criteria applicable to all state AYP policies — that is, measure achievement separately in reading/language arts and mathematics):

- they must incorporate an ultimate goal of all pupils reaching a proficient or higher level of achievement by the end of the 2013-2014 school year;
- achievement gaps among pupil groups must decline in order for schools or LEAs to meet AYP standards;
- annual achievement goals for pupils must not be set on the basis of pupil background or school characteristics;
- annual achievement goals must be based on performance standards, not past or "typical" performance growth rates;
- the assessment system must produce comparable results from grade-to-grade and year-to-year; and
- the progress of individual students must be tracked within a state data system.

In addition, applicant states must have their annual assessments for each of grades 3-8 approved by ED, and these assessments must have been in place for at least one year previous to implementation of the growth models.

In January 2006, ED published peer review guidance for growth model pilot applications.[21] In general, this guidance elaborates upon the requirements described above, with special emphasis on the following: (a) pupil growth targets may not consider their "race/ethnicity, socioeconomic status, school AYP status, or any other non-academic" factor; (b) growth targets are to be established on the basis of chievement standards, not typical growth patterns or past achievement; and (c) the state must have a longitudinal, individual pupil data system, capable of tracking pupils as they move among schools and LEAs within the state.

The requirements for growth models of AYP under this pilot are relatively restrictive. The models must be consistent with the ultimate goal of all pupils at a proficient or higher level by 2013-2014, a major goal of the statutory AYP provisions of NCLB. More significantly, they must incorporate comparable annual assessments, at least for each of grades 3-8 plus at least one senior high school year, and those assessments must be approved by ED and in place for at least one year before implementation of the growth model. Further, all performance expectations must be individualized, and the state must have an infrastructure of a statewide, longitudinal database for individual pupils. Proposed models would have to be structured around expectations and performance of individual pupils, not demographic groups of pupils in a school or LEA, although individual results would have to be aggregated for the demographic groups designated in NCLB.

According to ED, 20 states submitted applications to be allowed to use growth models to make AYP determinations beginning with either the 2005-2006 or 2006-2007 school years. Two states, North Carolina and Tennessee, were initially approved to use proposed growth models in making AYP determinations based on assessments administered in the 2005-2006 school year. Seven additional states —Arkansas, Delaware, Florida, Iowa, Ohio, Alaska, and Arizona — have been approved to participate in the pilot program subsequently, contingent in the case of Ohio on adoption of a uniform minimum group size for all pupil groups. The models for these nine states are briefly described below.

The *North Carolina* policy does not actually provide for a separate AYP model, but rather the addition of a projection component to the current group status model. If the achievement level of a non-proficient pupil is on a trajectory toward proficiency within four years, then the pupil is added to the proficient group. All other provisions of the current group status and successive group improvement models would continue to apply. Thus, the ultimate goal becomes: by the end of the 2013-2014 school year, all pupils will be either at a proficient or higher level, or on a four-year trajectory toward proficiency (without use of confidence intervals). The trajectory calculations will be made for pupils in the 3rd through 8th grades. SEA staff estimate that 4% of the schools in North Carolina that failed to meet AYP standards based on 2004-2005 assessment results would have met AYP standards if this growth model had been in place.

Under the *Tennessee* policy, schools and LEAs will have two options for meeting AYP: meeting either the AYP standards under the group status or successive group improvement models of current law, or meeting AYP standards according to a "projection model." Under the projection model, pupils are deemed to be at a proficient or higher level of achievement if their test scores are projected to be at a proficient or higher level three years into the future, based on past achievement levels for individual pupils. It should be noted that under this model, pupils who currently score at a proficient level, but who would be projected to score below a proficient level in three years, would not be counted as proficient. Further, the Tennessee growth/projection model implicitly assumes that pupils attend schools performing at a state average level. If, in actuality, they attend low-performing schools, their future achievement level may be overestimated.

Tennessee's projection model will not be applied to high schools. SEA staff estimate that 13% of the schools in Tennessee that failed to meet AYP standards based on 2004-2005 assessment results would have met AYP standards if this model had been in place.

Under the *Delaware* growth model, AYP will be calculated each year based on both the statutory provisions and using the state's growth model. A school will meet AYP standards if it qualifies using either method. Individual pupil performance will be tracked from one year to the next. Specified numbers of points (up to 300) will be awarded based on changes (if any) in pupils' performance level. Points will be awarded for partial movement toward proficiency, but the points awarded for movement to advanced levels beyond proficiency will be the same as for movement to proficiency. (Maintaining a level of proficient or higher awards 300 points as well.) The average growth scores for schools and LEAs to meet AYP standards increase steadily until 2013-2014, by which time all pupils would be expected to achieve at a proficient or higher level.[22]

Under the *Arkansas* policy, AYP will be calculated each year based on both statutory provisions and using the state's growth model. A school will meet AYP standards if it qualifies using either method. Under the growth model, pupils in grades 4-8 will be deemed to be proficient if they are on a growth path toward proficiency by the end of 8th grade. Pupils already proficient must be on a path to continue to be proficient through grade 8 (i.e., growth path criteria will be applied to all pupils, proficient and non-proficient). Individual annual proficiency thresholds and growth increments are designed to enable non-proficient students to reach proficiency by grade 8, and proficient students to continue to be proficient. Mobile pupils will be associated with the school they attended at the time of assessment administration in the previous year.

Under the *Florida* model, AYP will be determined separately for each pupil subgroup in each school or LEA (i.e., not for schools or LEAs as a whole) using the statutory models (status and safe harbor) plus a growth model. The school or LEA will meet AYP standards if each pupil subgroup makes AYP using one of the three models.

Florida's growth model will be essentially the same as the current status model, except that proficient pupils will include both those currently scoring at a proficient or higher level plus those who are on an individual path toward proficiency within three years. The combined percentage of pupils rated proficient will be compared to the standard AMO. The model will be applied to AYP determinations for grades 3-10 (with some modifications for pupils in grade 3). In its application, the Florida SEA estimated that for 2006-2007, 938 of the state's public schools would meet AYP standards with the growth model applied, compared to 743 schools without (out of a total of 3,200 schools).

Under the *Iowa* model, pupil tests score ranges below proficient have been divided into 3 categories: Hi Marginal, Lo Marginal, and Weak. A student who rises from one of these levels to a higher level, and has not previously attained the higher level, will be deemed to have met "Adequate Yearly Growth" (AYG). AYG is considered to be more than a typical year's growth over a one-year period. For schools and LEAs that have not met AYP though application of the standard status and safe harbor models, students making AYG will be added to those scoring proficient or above, and this combined total will be used in determining whether the school or LEA makes AYP for the year. Students scoring below the proficient level must continue to move to a higher sub-proficient level each year in order to be included in the combined proficient + AYG student count. This implies that students beginning at the "Weak" level must reach proficiency within three years, those beginning at Lo Marginal must become proficient within two years, and those beginning at Hi Marginal must reach proficiency within one year. By 2014, the growth model would no longer be used, and all pupils will be expected to achieve at a proficient or higher level.

Confidence intervals will continue to be applied to determine whether the combined proficient + AYG student count meets the required threshold to make AYP. This growth model will be applied statewide to test scores for grades 3-8 and 11, and to grades 9 and 10 as well in the LEAs that administer the Iowa Tests in those grades. The Iowa growth model does not currently include students with the most significant cognitive disabilities, who take the Iowa Alternate Assessment.

Ohio has adopted a variation of the "projection" or "on track to proficiency" approach that is common to the models for all of the other participating states except Delaware and Iowa. After application of the standard status and safe harbor models, if any pupil group fails to meet AYP, then a determination will be made if a sufficient proportion of pupils in the group is on track toward meeting the required proficiency threshold as of a "target grade." In the case of elementary and middle schools, the target grade will be either the grade level following the highest grade offered by the school (i.e., for a K-5 school, the 6th grade), or 4 grades beyond the pupil's current grade, whichever comes first. In the case of a high school, pupils would have to be on track toward proficiency by the 11th grade.

Pupils currently scoring at a proficient level but who are projected to be below the proficient level by the target grade will not be considered to be proficient in Ohio's projection model. Student achievement trajectories will be projected on an individual basis. Projections will be based on past test results (in all subjects, but with greater weight applied to past test results in the same subject) for each pupil.

Under *Alaska's* growth model, pupils will be included in the proficient group if their achievement level trajectory is on a growth path toward proficiency within 3 additional years for pupils in grades 4-9, or within 2 additional years for pupils in grade 10. (Alaska currently has no standards-based assessments for grades beyond 10.) Pupils in the third grade (the earliest grade at which state assessments are administered) will be measured based on status only, not growth. The growth model will not apply to pupils with disabilities who take alternate assessments. While Alaska had proposed that confidence intervals be applied, at a relatively low level (68%), under the growth model, the state agreed to drop this in the approved version. In its application, Alaska estimated that approximately 13% of pupils currently not proficient are on track toward proficiency, under the terms of the state's growth model.

Finally, in *Arizona*, the growth model will be applicable to pupils in grades 4-8 only. Pupils will be included in the proficient group if their achievement level trajectory is on a growth path toward proficiency within three years or by 8th grade, whichever comes first. Pupils in the third grade (the earliest grade at which state assessments are administered) will be measured based on status only, not growth. Unlike some other states participating in the growth model pilot, pupils with disabilities who take the state's alternate assessment (AIMS-A) will be included in the Arizona growth model. Such pupils with disabilities who move up one performance level (i.e., from "falls far below" to "approaches" or from "approaches" to "meets" the proficiency standard) will be deemed to have met their growth target.

Thus, most of the growth models approved under ED's pilot programs are based upon supplementing the number of pupils scoring at a proficient or higher level with those who are projected to be at a proficient level within a limited number of years. Seven of the nine approved models follow this general approach. Among these states, a distinction may be made between five states (North Carolina, Arkansas, Florida, Alaska, and Arizona) that combine currently proficient pupils with those not proficient who are "on track" toward proficiency, and two states (Tennessee and Ohio) that consider only projected proficiency levels for all pupils (i.e., currently proficient pupils who are not on track to remain proficient are counted as not proficient). In contrast, the models used by the other two states – Delaware and Iowa – focus on awarding credit for movement of pupils among achievement categories up to proficiency.

Bush Administration Reauthorization Proposal

On January 24, 2007, the Bush Administration released "Building on Results: A Blueprint for Strengthening the No Child Left Behind Act,"[23] which outlines its recommendations for ESEA reauthorization. Under this proposal, all participating states would be allowed to use growth models to make AYP determinations, subject to conditions comparable to those applicable to the current pilot program.

ISSUES REGARDING GROWTH MODEL ALTERNATIVES TO NCLB'S AYP MODELS

Why is there increased interest in growth models for determining AYP under NCLB? What might be the major advantages and disadvantages of growth models of AYP, in comparison to status or improvement models? These questions are addressed in the following pages.

Are Growth Models of AYP More Fair and Accurate than Status or Improvement Models?

Many proponents of growth models for school/LEA AYP see them as being more fair — to both pupils and school staff — and accurate than status or improvement models, primarily because they can be designed to take into consideration the currently widely varying levels of achievement of different pupil groups. Growth models generally recognize the reality that different schools and pupils have very different starting points in their achievement levels and recognize progress being made at all levels (e.g., from below basic to basic, or from proficient to advanced), giving credit for all improvements over previous performance.

Growth models would likely increase the ability to attribute pupil achievement to their current school, as opposed to their past schools or background characteristics, especially (but not only) if controls (and/or predicted growth elements) are included in the model. They more directly measure the effect of schools on the specific pupils they serve over a period of years, attempting to track the movement of pupils between schools and LEAs, rather than applying a single standard to all pupils in each state. They have the ability to focus on the specific effectiveness of schools and teachers with pupils whom they have actually taught for multiple years, rather than the change in performance of pupil groups among whom there has usually been a substantial amount of mobility. They can directly (as well as indirectly) adjust for non-school influences on achievement, comparing the same students across years and reducing errors due to student mobility.

Proponents of growth models often argue that status models of AYP in particular make schools and LEAs accountable for factors over which they have little control, and that status models focus insufficiently on pupil achievement gains, especially if those gains are below the threshold for proficient performance, or gains from a proficient to an advanced level. Status models, such as the current primary model of AYP under NCLB, might even create an undesirable incentive for teachers and schools to focus their attention, at least in the short run, on pupils who are only marginally below a proficient level of achievement, in hopes of bringing them above that sole key threshold, rather than the most disadvantaged pupils whose achievement is well below the proficient level. The current status model of AYP also confers no credit for achievement increases above the proficient level, that is, bringing pupils from the proficient to the advanced level.

At the same time, growth models of AYP have the significant disadvantage of implicitly setting lower thresholds or expectations for some pupil groups and/or schools. Although any growth model deemed consistent with NCLB would likely need to incorporate that act's ultimate goal of all pupils at a proficient or higher level of achievement by 2013-2014 (see below), the majority of such models used currently or in the past do not include such goals, and tend to allow disadvantaged schools and pupils to remain at relatively low levels of achievement for considerable periods of time.

Growth models of AYP may be quite complicated, and may address the accountability purposes of NCLB less directly and clearly than status or (to a lesser extent) improvement models. If the primary purpose of AYP is to determine whether schools and LEAs are succeeding at raising the achievement of their current pupils to challenging levels, with those goals and expectations applied consistently to all pupil groups, then the current provisions of NCLB might more simply and directly meet that purpose than growth model alternatives.

Pupil mobility among schools and LEAs is substantial, and has important implications for all models of AYP. However, its implications are multifaceted, and do not necessarily favor a particular AYP model. Growth models have the advantage of attempting to track pupils through longitudinal data systems. But if they thereby attribute the achievement of highly mobile pupils among a variety of schools and LEAs, accountability is dispersed. At the same time, the presence of highly mobile pupils in the groups considered in determining AYP under status and improvement models may seem unfair to school staff. However, the impact of such pupils in school-level AYP determinations is limited by NCLB's provision that pupils who have attended a particular school for less than one year need not be considered in such determinations.

Are Growth Models of Greater Value than Status or Improvement Models for Purposes Other than Accountability?

Growth models of AYP may offer increased value for purposes *other than* meeting the school and LEA accountability requirements of NCLB. These other purposes may include diagnosing pupil needs, conducting educational research, or pinpointing the specific impact of teachers, schools, or other educational resources on pupil achievement. These advantages derive largely, but not solely, from the incorporation of longitudinal pupil tracking systems within growth models.

Of course, current law does not prevent the use of growth models, under state authority, as a diagnostic/research/alternative accountability tool separate from the AYP and other requirements of NCLB. While the current statutory text and policy guidance associated with NCLB discourage the use of separate state and federal accountability systems for schools and LEAs,[24] they are not prohibited in practice, and separate accountability systems are currently being used by several states alongside the AYP system required by NCLB. Finally, the usefulness of a model of AYP for purposes *other than* accountability may be of limited relevance to a debate over whether such a model should be used for the accountability purposes of NCLB.

Do States Have Sufficient Resources to Develop and Implement Growth Models?

It is generally agreed that growth models of AYP are more demanding than status or improvement models in several respects, especially in terms of data requirements and analytical capacity. For a longitudinal data system sufficient to support a growth model, it is likely that states would need to have pupil data systems incorporating at least the following:

1. A unique statewide student identifier.
2. The ability to produce comparable results from grade to grade and from year to year (vertically-scaled assessments).
3. Student-level enrollment, demographic and program participation information.
4. Information on untested students.
5. Student level graduation and dropout data.
6. State-wide audit system.[25]

While the availability of information on state data systems is insufficient to enable one to determine with precision how many states could/could not currently implement such models if they chose to do so, it is very likely that growth models generally require resources and data systems that many states currently lack.[26]

This concern is being addressed in part through an ED program intended to help states design, develop, and implement statewide, longitudinal data systems. An initial appropriation of $24.8 million was provided for this program, administered by ED's Institute of Education Sciences (IES),[27] for FY2005, and $24.6 million for each of FY2006 and FY2007. The Administration has requested a substantial increase to $49.2 million for FY2008. Thus far, a total of 27 states have received awards through two rounds of competition.[28]

Under this program, aid is to be provided to state educational agencies (SEAs) via cooperative agreements, not grants, to allow increased federal involvement in the supported activities. According to the announcement in the April 15, 2005 *Federal Register*, the program is intended "to enable SEAs to design, develop, and implement statewide, longitudinal data systems to efficiently and accurately manage, analyze, disaggregate, and use individual student data.... Applications from states with the most limited ability to collect, analyze, and report individual student achievement data will have a priority...." According to ED, the program is designed to help SEAs meet the AYP and reporting requirements of NCLB, as well as to conduct value-added or achievement growth research, including "meaningful longitudinal analyses of student academic growth within all subgroups specified by the No Child Left Behind Act of 2001." There will also be an emphasis on encouraging data sharing among states, while at the same time protecting the security and privacy of data.

Are Growth Models Consistent with NCLB's Ultimate Goal?

The simple answer to this question is that most growth models used in the past or currently do not incorporate an ultimate goal such as the one under NCLB — that all pupils reach a proficient or higher level of achievement by 2013-2014 — but growth models could presumably be designed or modified to embody this element. Growth models of AYP generally incorporate one of two types of growth target, the "how much improvement is enough" aspect of the model: (a) data driven/predicted growth, or (b) policy driven/required growth targets. The first type of growth target has been most common, while NCLB's ultimate goal would represent a growth target of the second variety, with separate paths (with presumably separate starting points) for each relevant pupil cohort. Incorporating NCLB's ultimate goal into growth models might be technically difficult and inconsistent with the typical nature of such models in the past — with their orientation toward comparing achievement growth among a cohort of pupils with typical or predicted growth — but not impossible.

The models approved thus far under ED's growth model pilot arguably meet the ultimate goal requirement. However, under some of these models, pupils need only be proficient or *on track toward* proficiency within a limited number of years as of 2013-2014.

Would Use of Growth Models Likely Reduce the Number of Schools/Leas Identified as Failing to Meet AYP?

With the initial implementation of the provisions of NCLB, several thousand public schools and hundreds of LEAs have been identified each year as failing to meet state AYP standards.[29] It frequently appears to be implicitly assumed by potentially interested parties that widespread use of growth models of AYP would result in significantly smaller percentages of schools and LEAs being identified as failing to meet AYP standards. This view seems to be based largely on the assumption that differing starting points for various cohorts of pupils would involve lower starting points and initial AMOs for disadvantaged pupil groups, reducing the number of schools or LEAs that fail to meet AYP due to the performance of one or a few of such demographic groups.

Indeed, it is easy to hypothesize that during the first few years of implementation of growth models of AYP, required performance thresholds would be relatively low for disadvantaged pupil cohorts, and fewer schools or LEAs would fail to meet AYP standards. However, if one assumes that any AYP model under NCLB must meet that act's ultimate goal requirement, with regular increases in AMOs leading toward the ultimate goal of all pupils at a proficient or higher level by 2013-2014, any significant reduction in the number of schools or LEAs failing to make AYP would likely be temporary. This is particularly true because we are already several years into NCLB's presumed overall timeline of 2001-2002 (the "base year" for AYP determinations) to 2013-2014.

Of course, if it is assumed that use of growth models somehow improves the productivity of schools and LEAs — that is, by improving motivation of pupils or teachers, or by providing better diagnostic data on pupil achievement — then it is possible that this would ultimately reduce the number of schools/LEAs failing to meet AYP, but there is currently no direct proof that this would occur. As noted earlier, where estimates are available, the growth models approved for use under ED's pilot program would reduce the number of schools failing to meet AYP standards to a relatively limited degree.

Can Growth Models Be Applied at Grade Levels without Annual Assessments?

The value and usefulness of growth models of AYP are highly dependent on a regular flow of valid information on pupil achievement levels. As a result, it is frequently assumed that growth models can be appropriately implemented only when achievement test results, linked to a continuum of state content and performance standards, are available at least annually. This creates difficulties for implementing growth models across the entire K-12 grade span, since NCLB requires the administration of state standards-based assessments in each of grades 3-8, plus only one senior high school grade. It may be possible to fully implement growth models only over grade ranges for which annual assessment results are available. Substantial difficulties might be presented by the large degree of variation in curriculum, and frequently in assessments, for senior high school pupils, although that can present difficulties under any of the three types of AYP model.

References

[1] For general information on all aspects of the AYP concept in general, the No Child Left Behind Act provisions for AYP, and related issues, see CRS Report RL32495, *Adequate Yearly Progress (AYP): Implementation of the No Child Left Behind Act*, by Wayne Riddle.

[2] For more information on the pupil assessment requirements of the No Child Left Behind Act, see CRS Report RL31407, *Educational Testing: Implementation of ESEA Title I-A Requirements Under the No Child Left Behind Act*, by Wayne Riddle.

[3] For a discussion of these consequences and corrective actions, see CRS Report RL31487, *Education for the Disadvantaged: Overview of ESEA Title I-A Amendments Under the No Child Left Behind Act*, by Wayne Riddle; and CRS Report RL33506, *School Choice Under the ESEA: Programs and Requirements*, by David Smole.

[4] There is a variant of the group status model, sometimes called an "index model," under which partial credit would be attributed to performance improvements below the proficient level — e.g., from below basic to basic.

[5] Scores may be combined for pupils in all assessed grade levels in a school.

[6] One state, Massachusetts, has injected a partial growth element into its safe harbor provision. In that state, a school or LEA that fails to meet the standard AYP requirements still makes AYP if the number of pupils in relevant groups and subjects scoring below the proficient level declines by 10% or more from the previous year *or* declines sufficiently to put them on track toward proficiency by the end of the 2013-2014 school year.

[7] See, for example, *Issues in the Design of Accountability Systems*, by Robert L. Linn, CSE Technical Report 650, National Center for Research on Evaluation, Standards, and Student Testing, April 2005.

[8] It has occasionally been said that the AYP systems approved by ED for a few states before initiation of the growth model pilot announced in November 2005 incorporate "growth" elements. However, such claims appear to be based primarily on the inclusion

in the AYP systems of "pupil achievement indexes" (i.e., the "index models" referred to in the first footnote under the section "The Range of Possible Models for Measuring AYP for Schools and LEAs," above) that give partial credit for achievement gains below the proficient level, comparing this year's pupil groups with last year's. They do not meet the definition of growth model as used in this report.

[9] This is determined by ranking all public schools (of the relevant grade level) statewide according to their percentage of pupils at the proficient or higher level of achievement (based on all pupils in each school), and setting the threshold at the point where one-fifth of the schools (weighted by enrollment) have been counted, starting with the schools at the lowest level of achievement.

[10] Under program regulations [34 C.F.R. § 200.16(c)(2)], the starting point may vary by grade span (e.g., elementary, middle, etc.) and subject.

[11] This secondary AYP provision of NCLB is sometimes referred to as a "growth model," but it is not consistent with that term as used in this report, in part because it is based on pupil group averages, and not the longitudinal performance of individual pupils in a cohort.

[12] As noted earlier, under the accountability policy approved for use in Massachusetts, a school or LEA also meets the safe harbor requirement if the number of pupils in relevant groups and subjects scoring below the proficient level declines sufficiently to put them on track toward proficiency by the end of the 2013-2014 school year.

[13] Under NCLB, state AYP systems must include at least one indicator, other than achievement test scores. For senior high schools, the additional indicator must be the graduation rate. A typical additional indicator for elementary and middle schools is the attendance rate.

[14] The Senate-passed bill would have authorized states to use index systems with a limited growth-related element — under an index system, states could have combined different demographic groups of pupils, with greater weight applied to pupils whose level of achievement was initially furthest below the proficient level.

[15] During the immediate pre-NCLB period, a few states identified schools as failing to make AYP if they failed to meet "expected growth" in performance based on factors such as initial achievement levels and statewide average achievement trends. The "growth" models used by states in the pre-NCLB period were generally much closer in structure to the successive group improvement model, as described in this report, than to the individual/cohort growth model.

[16] As noted earlier, the "safe harbor" provision requires a 10% reduction in the percentage of relevant pupils whose performance is below the proficient level. For a pupil group currently at 20%, this would require an increase in 8 percentage points (to 28%), but for a group currently at 80%, this would require an increase of only 2 percentage points (to 82%).

[17] See *Issues in the Design of Accountability Systems*, by Robert L. Linn, CSE Technical Report 650, National Center for Research on Evaluation, Standards, and Student Testing, April 2005.

[18] Readers may also wish to consult a Government Accountability Office (GAO) report published in July 2006: "No Child Left Behind Act: States Face Challenges Measuring Academic Growth That Education's Initiatives May Help Address," GAO-06-661.

[19] It is sometimes said that "index" systems incorporated into the AYP standards of three states (Massachusetts, Minnesota, and Oklahoma) constitute "growth model elements" allowed by ED under current law. However, the distinctive element of these AYP standards is the use of indexes that give partial credit for achievement gains at levels below proficient (such as moving from below basic to basic). Such provisions have been allowed by ED, at least for these three states, with the additional criteria that AYP must be calculated separately for each required subject area and subgroup, incorporate the goal of all pupils at a proficient or higher level of achievement by 2013-2014, not give extra credit for moving beyond proficient, have AMOs, and not allow a school to make AYP without increasing the number of students at the proficient level over the previous year.

[20] See [http://www.ed.gov/news/pressreleases/2005/11/11182005.html].

[21] See [http://www.ed.gov/policy/elsec/guid/growthmodelguidance.pdf].

[22] Delaware's proposal included the use of confidence intervals at an unspecified level in implementing the growth model; however, ED approved use of the model without confidence intervals.

[23] The document is available from the Department of Education at [http://www.ed.gov/policy/elsec/leg/nclb/buildingonresults.pdf].

[24] For example, NCLB provides that "Each [participating] State shall demonstrate that the State has developed and is implementing a single, statewide State accountability system...." Nevertheless, several states have continued to administer separate accountability systems, authorized under state law, while also implementing the AYP provisions of NCLB.

[25] Aimee Guidera, director of the Data Quality Campaign, as quoted in: Commission on No Child Left Behind, Commission Staff Research Report, "Growth Models: An examination within the context of NCLB," August 2006, available at [http://www.aspeninstitute.org/ atf/cf/{DEB6F227-659B-4EC8-8F84-8DF23CA704F5}/Growth%20Models%20and% 20NCLB%20Report.pdf], visited on September 6, 2006.

[26] According to a March 16, 2005, Memo from the Council of Chief State School Officers [http://www.ccsso.org/content/pdfs/Growthmemo.pdf], about half of the states have "statewide individual student record data systems" necessary to implement growth models of AYP.

[27] This program is authorized by Section 208 of the Education Sciences Reform Act of 2002, P.L. 107-279. The authorized funding level is $80 million for FY2003 and "such sums as may be necessary" for each of the succeeding five fiscal years.

[28] For additional information, see [http://nces.ed.gov/Programs/SLDS/].

[29] See CRS Report RL32495, Adequate Yearly Progress (AYP): Implementation of the No Child Left Behind Act, by Wayne C. Riddle.

In: No Child Left Behind: Issues and Developments
Editor: P. H. Berkhart, pp. 55-81
ISBN: 978-1-60456-210-1

Chapter 3

MONTGOMERY GI BILL EDUCATION BENEFITS: ANALYSIS OF COLLEGE PRICES AND FEDERAL STUDENT AID UNDER THE HIGHER EDUCATION ACT*

Charmaine Mercer and Rebecca R. Skinner

ABSTRACT

Educational assistance programs have been authorized for veterans of the Armed Forces since 1944. The Servicemen's Readjustment Act of 1944 (P.L. 78346), or the GI Bill of Rights, provided support, including education benefits, to veterans of World War II. Subsequently, other programs were implemented for similar purposes (e.g., the Korean GI Bill and the Vietnam Era GI Bill). These new programs were primarily, if not exclusively, funded by the federal government and were intended to support veterans returning from war. The implementation of the Post-Vietnam Era Veterans' Educational Assistance Program (VEAP) marked the first time that an educational benefit had been established for an all-volunteer force, serving during a period of peace; the first time that education benefits were viewed as a recruiting tool for the military; and the first time that program participants were required to contribute to the education benefit fund while in the military. Many of the principles of VEAP were carried over during the creation of the Montgomery GI Bill (MGIB), the current military education benefit that was implemented in 1985.

Military education benefits have evolved significantly over the last 60-plus years. For example, military education benefits initially were completely subsidized by the federal government; they were issued to institutions of higher education (IHEs) on behalf of the veteran; and the benefits included subsistence payments and could be used for numerous training and educational programs. Conversely, the current benefits are partially subsidized, paid directly to the student as a subsistence payment, and are limited to specific training and education programs. College prices have substantially changed during this period. For example, in a recent 20-year period (academic years 1985-1986 to 2005-2006), the average tuition, fees, room, and board at a four-year public institution increased by 214% (current dollars). Moreover, the manner in which federal student

* Excerpted from CRS Report RL33281, dated January 19, 2007.

financial aid is calculated and awarded has shifted several times during the evolution of the military education benefits program. At present, federal student assistance is calculated according to the federal need analysis system, which considers the receipt of military education benefits when determining eligibility for some student aid programs. These policy and program changes have altered the role that military benefits play in providing access to postsecondary education for veterans.

This report provides information about the various military education benefits provided to members of the Armed Forces and how these benefits have changed over time. More specifically, it includes a historical overview of education benefits for military veterans, an analysis of the estimated value of these benefits with respect to the average college price, and a discussion of the interaction between military education benefits and federal student aid benefits authorized by Title IV of the Higher Education Act of 1965 (HEA), as amended.

Key Staff for Military Education Benefits and Postsecondary Education

Area of Expertise	Name	Telephone
Military Education Benefits, General	Charmaine Mercer	7-4894
Federal Student Aid	Charmaine Mercer Rebecca R. Skinner	7-4894 7-6600
Federal Student Aid Need Analysis	Charmaine Mercer	7-4894
College Prices	Rebecca R. Skinner	7-6600

Congress has demonstrated an interest since 1944 in providing education benefits to members of the Armed Forces. The Servicemen's Readjustment Act of 1944 (P.L. 78-346), or the GI Bill of Rights, provided support, including education benefits, to veterans of World War II. Following the expiration of the original GI Bill, other programs were implemented for similar purposes including the Korean GI Bill, Vietnam Era GI Bill, the Post-Vietnam Era Veterans' Educational Assistance Program (VEAP), and the current GI Bill, the Montgomery GI Bill (MGIB). These new programs were primarily, if not exclusively, funded by the federal government and were intended to support veterans returning from war. While various differences exist between the programs, the two more recent programs, VEAP and MGIB, have required participants to make contributions toward their education benefits while in the military, whereas previous programs did not include this requirement. Given the ongoing military conflicts in Iraq and Afghanistan and the substantial number of military personnel and reservists that have been called to active duty, there is renewed congressional interest in the education benefits available to members of the Armed Forces through the MGIB.

Military education benefits have evolved significantly over the last 60-plus years. For example, military education benefits initially were completely subsidized by the federal government; they were issued to institutions of higher education (IHEs) on behalf of the veteran; and the benefits included subsistence payments and could be used for numerous training and educational programs. Conversely, the current benefits are partially subsidized, paid directly to the student as a subsistence payment, and are limited to specific training and education programs. College prices have substantially changed during this period. For example, in a recent 20-year period (academic year 1985-1986 to 2005-2006), the average tuition, fees, room, and board at a four-year public institution increased by 214% (current dollars). Over the same time period, MGIB-Active Duty (discussed in this report) monthly benefits increased by 175%. Moreover, the manner in which federal student financial aid is calculated and awarded has shifted several times during the evolution of the military education benefits program. At present, federal student assistance is calculated according to the federal need analysis system, which considers the receipt of military education benefits when determining eligibility for some student aid programs (discussed in this report). These policy and program changes made by Congress have altered the role that military benefits play in providing access to postsecondary education for veterans.

This report provides information about the various military education benefits provided to members of the Armed Forces and how these benefits have changed over time. The report is organized into three major sections. Section One provides a historical overview of education benefits for military veterans. The overview begins with the Servicemen's Readjustment Act of 1944 (GI Bill of Rights) and continues through the current Montgomery GI Bill. The second section is an analysis of the estimated value of these benefits with respect to the average college price. This section focuses on the estimated value of veterans' education benefits and college prices at four-year public and private institutions and two-year public institutions. The final section examines the interaction between military education benefits and federal student aid benefits authorized by Title IV of the Higher Education Act of 1965 (HEA), as amended. It includes short descriptions of the Title IV student aid programs, an overview of the federal student aid need analysis formula that is used to determine the amount a family is expected to contribute to the costs of higher education, and an examination of how the formula treats military education benefits.

Historical Overview of Benefits Provided through the GI Bill[1]

GI Bill of Rights

The original GI Bill, the Servicemen's Readjustment Act of 1944, was intended to help veterans readjust to civilian life, avoid high levels of unemployment, and afford returning veterans an opportunity to receive the education and training that they missed while serving in the military. Under the GI Bill, the Veterans Administration, now the Department of Veterans Affairs (VA), paid up to $500 a year directly to an educational institution for tuition, books, fees, and other training costs.[2] The VA also paid as much as $50 a month (increased to $65 in 1946 and $75 in 1948) as a subsistence allowance to single veterans and a greater monthly amount to veterans with one or more dependents. This program ended on July 25, 1956.

Korean GI Bill

The Veterans' Readjustment Assistance Act of 1952, the Korean GI Bill (P.L. 82-550), was authorized to help veterans returning from the Korean war to adjust to civilian life. The benefit provided up to $100 a month for educational expenses and education-related expenses. Unlike the GI Bill of Rights, which paid both educational expenses and a subsistence allowance, the monthly benefit for the Korean GI Bill was intended to cover both. It was believed that requiring the veteran to contribute to the costs of his/her education would encourage more careful spending. In addition, partially in response to alleged incidents of fraud and abuse by for-profit (proprietary) IHEs, each veteran received a lump-sum payment from the VA instead of the VA making direct payments to IHEs.

Post-Korea and Vietnam-Era GI Bill

The Veterans' Readjustment Benefits Act, the Post-Korea and Vietnam-Era GI Bill (P.L.89-358), was enacted in 1966. This program was originally intended for veterans of the post-Korean war era, and was not intended to be as generous as some of the earlier programs for veterans.[3] Under this act, veterans who had been on active duty for more than 180 consecutive days were entitled to one month of educational assistance for each month of service. This was the first GI Bill that provided benefits to members of the Armed Forces while they served on active duty, as opposed to providing benefits only after the completion of active duty.

Post-Vietnam Era Veterans' Educational Assistance Program (VEAP)

The Post-Vietnam Era Veterans' Educational Assistance Program (VEAP), which was established by Title IV of the Veterans' Education and Employment Assistance Act of 1976 (P.L. 94-502), was considered an effective recruitment incentive for the Armed Forces during peacetime. Because the benefit was established for an all-volunteer force serving during peacetime, it was deemed appropriate to require participants, for the first time, to contribute to an education fund while in the military. Program participants had to agree to monthly pay reductions of at least $25 but not more than $100. The maximum education benefit could not exceed the amount contributed by the participant and the matching federal contribution (see table 1 for details).[4]

Montgomery GI Bill

The Montgomery GI Bill (MGIB), originally called the All-Volunteer Force Educational Assistance Program, was initially enacted as part of the Department of Defense Authorization Act, 1985 (P.L. 98-525), as a three-year pilot program.[5] Similar to its predecessors and incorporating many of the principles of the VEAP program, the MGIB is intended to provide educational assistance to individuals who have served in the Armed Forces and are attempting to readjust to civilian life. In addition, the benefit is intended to aid in the recruitment and retention of qualified personnel for the Armed Forces.

The MGIB consists of two major programs: MGIB-Active Duty (MGIB-AD) for individuals who are on active duty or after separation from active duty and MGIB-Selected Reserves (MGIB-SR) for members of the selected reserves. Another program, the Reserve Educational Assistance Program (REAP),[6] provides benefits for members of reserve components who are called or ordered to active duty in response to a war or national emergency as declared by the President or Congress. Each of these programs shares the common purpose of providing education benefits to members of the Armed Services, but there are distinct differences in the eligibility criteria, benefits provided, and contribution amounts (see table 1).

DATA ANALYSIS

The data for military education benefits presented in this report are derived primarily from the U.S. Department of Veterans Affairs. It is important to note that these benefits are generally awarded for a specific number of months, depending upon the program, when the recipient enrolled, and the duration of service. For example, a recipient can receive MGIB benefits for 36 months, which could be disbursed over the course of three years (one payment times 12 months) or over the course of four years [one payment times nine months (the number of months in an academic year)].[7] The analyses presented in this report assume that the benefits will be disbursed over a four-year period.

Most of the college price data are from the *Digest of Education Statistics, 2004* (*Digest*), produced by the Department of Education (ED). The analyses using college prices are limited because the Digest only provides college price data for the academic years 1964-1965 through 2003-2004. Further, the format for collecting data changed in the academic year 1975-1976; prior to this, the average tuition, fees, room, and board values reported were for four-year universities, not all four-year institutions.[8] In addition, data for 2004-2005 and 2005-2006 are from the College Board because these data are not currently available from ED. It should be noted that the College Board bases its college price data on a sample of institutions, whereas ED includes the universe of IHEs in its price data.

COMPARISON OF EDUCATION BENEFITS OVER TIME

The education benefits available through the GI Bill have changed since the inception of the GI Bill program. Byadjustingbenefits for inflation (price increases), it is possible to compare the actual (real) value of these different benefits over time. This analysis only considers available benefits for education and living expenses. It does not factor in any contributions toward those education benefits that veterans began making with the passage of the VEAP in 1976 or "kickers" provided to encourage enrollment in the Armed Forces. In addition, it only considers benefits available to full-time students with no dependents.[9] This section examines the value of the education benefits provided through the GI Bill (collectively referred to hereafter as the GI Bill) and subsequent programs from 1944 through 2005 in inflation-adjusted (constant) 2005 dollars. For the MGIB, only education benefits provided through the MGIB-AD program are included. It also considers the purchasing power of these education benefits with respect to attending a four-year public or private institution, or a two-year public institution.

Table 1. Program Eligibility Requirements for Military Education Benefits

Criteria	GI Bill of Rights	Korean GI Bill	Vietnam- Era GI Bill	Post-Vietnam Era Veterans' Educational Assistance Program (VEAP)	Montgomery GI Bill — Active Duty	Montgomery GI Bill — Selected Reserves	Reserve Educational Assistance Program (REAP)
Year enacted	1944	1952	1966	1976	1984	1984	2004
Initial authorization	P.L. 78-346	P.L. 82-550	P.L. 89-358	P.L. 94-502	P.L. 98-525	P.L. 98-525	P.L. 108-375
Highest benefit amount (current dollars)	$500 per year maximum; and $75 monthly subsistence	$110 per month maximum	$376 per month	Maximum benefit: $8,100[a]	$1,034 per month (FY2006)[b]	$297 per month (FY2006)[b]	$827.20 per month (FY2006)[c]
Duration of benefits	One year full-time training plus a period equal to time in service; 48 months maximum	1.5 times the duration of active service; 36 months maximum	One month of education benefits for every month of active duty service; 45 months maximum	Lesser of 36 months or number of months of contributions	Lesser of 36 months or number of months of active duty	36 months	36 months
Contribution	None	None	None	$25 to $100 per month; $2,700 maximum	Pay reduction of $100 per month for the first 12 months of pay	None	None
Length of service	Minimum 90 days	Minimum 90 days	More than 180 days of active duty service	Minimum 181 continuous days of active duty service, if entered before October 16, 1981; 24 months of continuous active duty service if entered after October 16, 1981	Minimum 181 continuous days of active duty service; 24 months of active duty if enlisted after September 7, 1980	Accepted 6-year reserve obligation after June 30, 1985	90 days of consecutive service in a contingency operation

Table 1. (Continued).

Criteria	GI Bill of Rights	Korean GI Bill	Vietnam- Era GI Bill	Post-Vietnam Era Veterans' Educational Assistance Program (VEAP)	Montgomery GI Bill — Active Duty	Montgomery GI Bill — Selected Reserves	Reserve Educational Assistance Program (REAP)
Period of service	September 16, 1940, through July 25, 1947	June 27, 1950, through January 31, 1955	February 1, 1955 through August 4, 1964 (Post-Korean War); August 5, 1964, through May 7, 1975 (Vietnam-Era veterans)	December 31, 1976, through July 1, 1985	Entered active duty after June 30, 1985	July 1, 1985, to present	After September 11, 2001, to present
Discharge status	Other than dishonorable	Other than dishonorable	Other than dishonorable	Other than dishonorable	Fully honorable discharge	Must remain with Reserve unit	Must remain with Reserve unit
Time limitation on use of benefits	Initiated by later of end of war or two years after discharge	Initiated by three years and completed by eight years after discharge	Within 8 years after discharge; 10 years for Vietnam veterans	Within 10 years of discharge or release from active duty	Within 10 years of discharge or release from active duty	Within 14 years of initial eligibility, if eligible on or after October 1, 1992 — prior to October 1, 1992, benefits must be used within 10 years of initial eligibility	Benefits can be used after 90-day minimum service period completed — no fixed delimited date; must remain with Reserve component

Table 1. (Continued).

Criteria	GI Bill of Rights	Korean GI Bill	Vietnam- Era GI Bill	Post-Vietnam Era Veterans' Educational Assistance Program (VEAP)	Montgomery GI Bill — Active Duty	Montgomery GI Bill — Selected Reserves	Reserve Educational Assistance Program (REAP)
Period of Use	June 22, 1944, to July 25, 1956	August 20, 1952, to January 31, 1965	June 1, 1966, to December 31, 1989	January 1, 1977, to present	July 1, 1985, to present	July 1, 1985, to present	December 9, 2001, to present

Source: Table prepared by CRS based on data available from the U.S. Department of Veterans Affairs.

a. Government matches every $1 the service person contributes with $2. The maximum benefit available under the program is $8,100 ($5,400 federal contribution and $2,700 individual contribution). The total contribution (service person contribution plus government share) is then divided by the number of months the service person contributed to VEAP.

b. Amounts shown are for full-time institutional training, and are for individuals who completed a minimum of three years of service. The amounts are less for individuals who served less than three years and who attend less than full-time. The education benefits payment rate schedule is available at [http://www.gibill.va.gov/GI_Bill_Info/rates.htm].

c. The monthly amount is a percentage of the MGIB-Active Duty and is based on the number of continuous days of active duty service. The amount shown is for full-time institutional training, and is for individuals who completed at least two years or more of active duty service. The amount is less for individuals who served less than two years, and who attend less than full-time.

Value of Education Benefits Provided through the GI Bill: 19442005

As previously discussed, the original GI Bill provided up to $500 annually for education expenses. This is the equivalent of an estimated $5,548 in 2005 dollars.[10] An additional $50 was provided monthly for living expenses in 1944, which is equivalent to $555 monthly, or $4,995 annually in 2005 dollars.[11] Thus, the total education benefit, including the living allowance, in 1944 would have been worth $10,543 annually, or $1,176 monthly in 2005 dollars.[12] Subsequent GI Bills provided benefits on a monthly basis.[13] In 1952, the year the Korean GI Bill was enacted, the education benefit was $131 per month, which is equal to $965 per month in real-dollar 2005 terms. When the Vietnam-Era GI bill was enacted in 1966, the monthly benefit dropped in both current dollars and constant dollars. With the inception of the program, the monthly benefit dropped from $110 in 1965 to $100 in 1966.[14] The latter is equivalent to $603 in constant 2005 dollars. As previously discussed, the Vietnam-Era education benefit was not intended to be as generous as its predecessors. In 1985, the year the MGIBwas implemented, the monthly benefit was $376, or $682 in constant 2005 dollars.

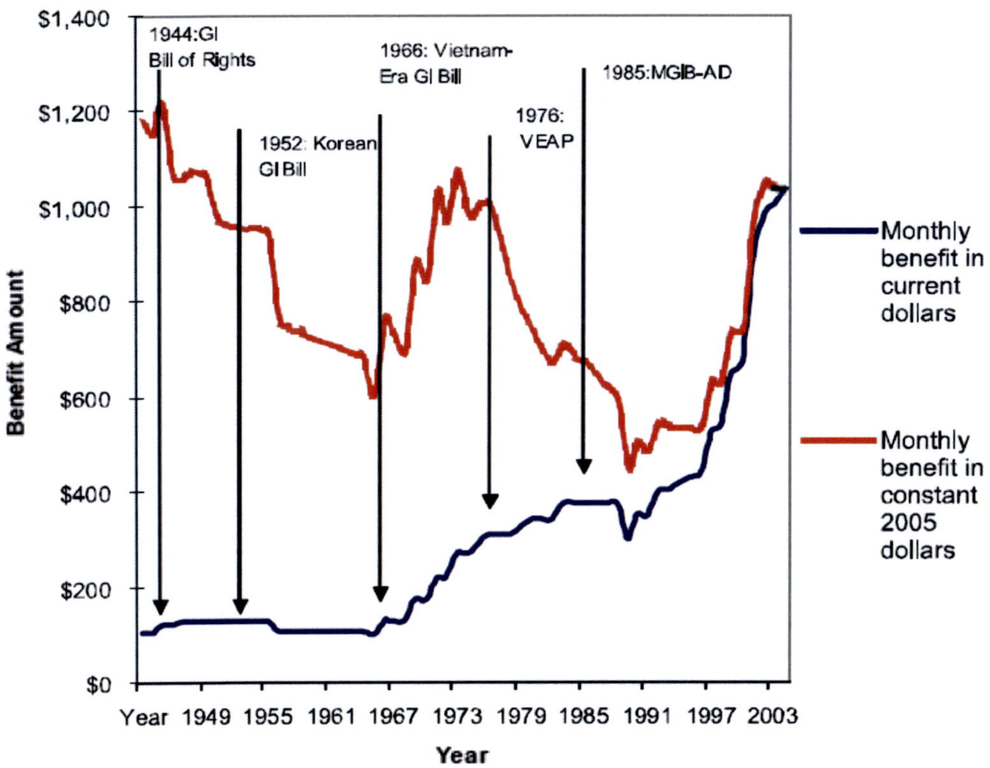

Source: Table prepared by CRS based on data from the U.S. Department of Veterans Affairs and U.S. Bureau of Labor Statistics.

Note: All constant dollar calculations are based on the average Consumer Price Index-All Urban Consumers (CPI-U) for each year. Monthly education benefits include any funds available for living expenses. All dollar amounts have been rounded.

Figure 1. GI Monthly Education Benefits in Current and Constant Dollars: 1944-2005.

Although the nominal value of the monthly benefits has significantly increased since the inception of the GI Bill, rising from $106 per month in 1944 to $1,034 per month in 2005, the period was marked by substantial fluctuations in the benefit's purchasing power (see figure 1). As illustrated in figure 1, the value of the benefits in constant dollars dropped during the 1950s and 1980s, but greatly increased during the early to mid 1970s and late 1990s.

Value of Education Benefits Provided through the Montgomery GI Bill: 1985-2005

Table 2 illustrates the education benefit provided by the Montgomery GI Bill from the program's inception in 1985 to 2005, and calculates its value in constant 2005 dollars. All benefits include any allowances for living expenses. For each year the amount shown is the highest basic benefit payable to a single veteran for any month and under any program in effect during that year.

Table 2. GI Bill Monthly Education Benefits in Current Dollars and Constant 2005 Dollars: 1985-2005

Year	Monthly benefit in current dollars	Monthly benefit in constant 2005 dollars
1985	$376	$682
1986	$376	$670
1987	$376	$646
1988	$376	$621
1989	$376	$592
1990	$300	$448
1991	$350	$502
1992	$350	$487
1993	$400	$541
1994	$405	$534
1995	$417	$534
1996	$428	$533
1997	$440	$535
1998	$528	$633
1999	$536	$628
2000	$650	$737
2001	$672	$741
2002	$900	$977
2003	$985	$1,045
2004	$1,004	$1,038
2005	$1,034	$1,034

Source: Table created by CRS based on data provided by the U.S. Department of Veterans Affairs and the U.S. Bureau of Labor Statistics.

Note: All constant dollar calculations are based on the average Consumer Price Index-All Urban Consumers (CPI-U) for each year. Monthly education benefits include any funds available for living expenses. All dollar amounts have been rounded.

Any additional payments or "kickers" provided by DOD are excluded.[15] Based on the benefit amounts in table 2, it is clear that the value of the Montgomery GI Bill has changed over the last 20 years. Until recently, the constant-dollar education benefit provided under the MGIB was not as generous as those provided in the 1970s (as shown in figure 1). Even at its most generous benefit levels in 2003-2005, the MGIB has not provided the same level of inflation-adjusted benefits as provided under the original GI Bill.[16]

Purchasing Power of the Montgomery GI Bill

It is also useful to consider how much education the current benefit, the Montgomery GI Bill, has "bought" since the program began. That is, looking at the average price of attending a four-year public or private institution, or a two-year public institution, how much did the MGIB cover? The following analysis examines the purchasing power of the GI Bill from the academic years 1985-1986 through 2005-2006. The analysis considers what percentage of tuition, fees, room, and board the MGIB benefit covered on an annual basis at four-year public and private institutions, as well as at two-year public institutions.[17]

As shown in table 3, since the inception of the MGIB program in 1985, the benefits have covered less than 100% of the average tuition, fees, room, and board at four-year public institutions. In academic year 1985-1986, the benefit covered approximately 88% of these expenses at a four-year public institution, and about 77% of the average price during the 2005-2006 academic year despite increases in the monthly benefit over this time period. From 1985-1986 to 2005-2006, monthly education benefits increased by 175%, while the price of attendance increased by 214%. For the 2005-2006 academic year, recipients would have needed an additional $2,821 to pay for their average annual tuition, fees, room, and board at a public four-year institution.

The MGIB benefits have covered even less of these expenses at four-year private institutions. The education benefits peaked at 37% of the average tuition, fees, room, and board at a four-year private institution in 1985-1986 and did not again exceed 30% until 2002-2003 (table 3). In addition, because the rate of increase in the average price of attendance was comparable to that at public four-year institutions, individuals who attended a four-year private institution would have needed an additional $19,720 to cover the costs of the average tuition, fees, room, and board during the 2005-2006 academic year.

Historically the benefits have been most generous at two-year public institutions, which, on average, tend to have a lower price of attendance and a smaller increase in prices (table 3). With the exception of the 1990s, the MGIB benefits have covered more than 100% of the average tuition, fees, room, and board at two-year public institutions. In addition, the increase in the average price of attendance at these institutions from 1985-1986 to 2005-2006 was 101%, substantially below the rate of increase at four-year public and private institutions. For the most recent academic year for which data are available (2003-2004), MGIB recipients who attended two-year public institutions would have had $2,879 remaining after paying tuition, fees, room, and board.

Table 3. Percent of Average Price of Four-Year Public and Private Institutions and Two-Year Public Institutions Covered by the GI Education Benefit: 1985-1986 through 2005-2006 (in current dollars)

Academic Year	Monthly MGIB benefit	Annual MGIB benefit (nine month academic year)	Four-year public institutions		Four-year private institutions		Two-year public institutions	
			Average tuition, fees, room, and board	Percent of price covered by benefit	Average tuition, fees, room, and board	Percent of price covered by benefit	Average tuition, fees, room, and board	Percent of price covered by benefit
1985-1986	$376	$3,384	$3,859	87.7%	$9,228	36.7%	$2,981	113.5%
1986-1987	$376	$3,384	$4,138	81.8%	$10,039	33.7%	$2,989	113.2%
1987-1988	$376	$3,384	$4,403	76.9%	$10,659	31.7%	$3,066	110.4%
1988-1989	$376	$3,384	$4,678	72.3%	$11,474	29.5%	$3,183	106.3%
1989-1990	$376	$3,384	$4,975	68.0%	$12,284	27.5%	$3,299	102.6%
1990-1991	$300	$2,700	$5,243	51.5%	$13,237	20.4%	$3,467	77.9%
1991-1992	$350	$3,150	$5,693	55.3%	$14,258	22.1%	$3,623	87.0%
1992-1993	$350	$3,150	$6,020	52.3%	$15,009	21.0%	$3,799	82.9%
1993-1994	$400	$3,600	$6,365	56.6%	$15,904	22.6%	$3,996	90.1%
1994-1995	$405	$3,645	$6,670	54.6%	$16,602	22.0%	$4,137	88.1%
1995-1996	$417	$3,753	$7,014	53.5%	$17,612	21.3%	$4,217	89.0%
1996-1997	$428	$3,852	$7,334	52.5%	$18,442	20.9%	$4,404	87.5%
1997-1998	$440	$3,960	$7,673	51.6%	$19,070	20.8%	$4,509	87.8%
1998-1999	$528	$4,752	$8,027	59.2%	$19,929	23.8%	$4,604	103.2%
1999-2000	$536	$4,824	$8,275	58.3%	$20,706	23.3%	$4,720	102.2%
2000-2001	$650	$5,850	$8,653	67.6%	$21,856	26.8%	$4,839	120.9%
2001-2002	$672	$6,048	$9,196	65.8%	$22,896	26.4%	$5,137	117.7%
2002-2003	$900	$8,100	$9,787	82.8%	$23,787	34.1%	$5,601	144.6%
2003-2004	$985	$8,865	$10,720	82.7%	$25,204	35.2%	$5,986	148.1%
2004-2005	$1,004	$9,036	$11,376	79.6%	$27,465	32.9%	na	na
2005-2006	$1,034	$9,306	$12,127	76.7%	$29,026	32.1%	na	na

Source: Table prepared by CRS based on data provided by the Department of Veterans Affairs, data available from the U.S. Department of Education, National Center for Education Statistics (NCES), *Digest of Education Statistics: 2004*, table 313, and data available from The College Board, *Trends in College Pricing: 2005*.

Note: Monthly education benefits include any funds available for living expenses. The annual MGIB education benefit is based on nine months of education benefits to coincide with a nine-month academic year. All dollar amounts have been rounded.

na: Not available.

GI Bill Benefits and Purchasing Power: A Historical View

The benefits provided under previous GI Bill programs are purported to have been more generous than the current benefits. Figures 2 through 4 detail how GI Bill benefits have fared historically in comparison with postsecondary tuition, fees, room, and board. Reliable national data on the price of college are not available prior to the 1964-1965 academic year; therefore, the data presented are limited to the academic years 1964-1965 to 2005-2006. As the analysis assumes a nine-month academic year, monthly education benefits were multiplied accordingly.

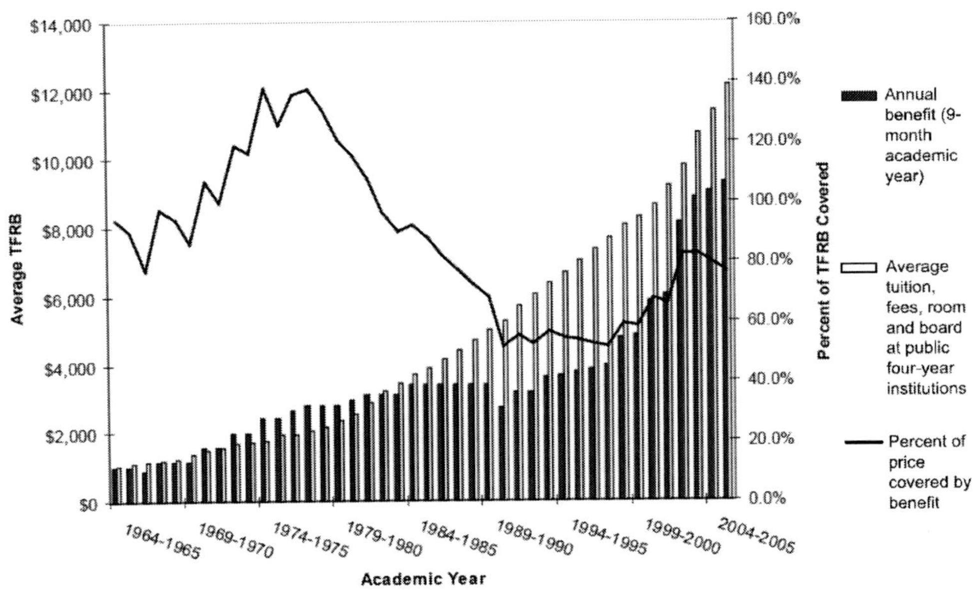

Source: Table prepared by CRS based on data provided by the Department of Veterans Affairs; data available from the U.S. Department of Education, National Center for Education Statistics (NCES), *Digest of Education Statistics: 2004*, table 313; and data available from The College Board, *Trends in College Pricing: 2005*. Note: Monthly education benefits include any funds available for living expenses. The annual MGIB education benefit is based on nine months of education benefits to coincide with a nine-month academic year. All dollar amounts have been rounded.

Figure 2. Percentage of Average Tuition, Fees, Room and Board (TFRB) of Four-Year Public Institutions Covered by GI Bill Education Benefit: 1964-1965 through 2005-2006.

As illustrated by figure 2, the GI Bill benefits covered a greater percentage of the average tuition, fees, room, and board at a four-year public institution in academic year 1964-1965 than they do currently. Prior to the 1985 enactment of the current education benefit program, the benefits never covered less than 86% of the average price, and in some instances covered as much as 138%. Figure 2 also demonstrates that tuition, fees, room, and board at four-year public institutions have increased at a greater rate than the GI Bill benefits. More specifically, with the exception of the 1970s and 1980s, tuition, fees, room, and board have exceeded the annual GI Bill benefits. For example, from academic year 2000-2001 to 2005-2006, the MGIB benefits have covered approximately 66% to 83% of the average tuition, fees, room, and board at four-year public institutions.

An examination of historical data on education benefits and the percentage of expenses they covered at four-year private and two-year public institutions reveals similar patterns to those identified from 1985-1986 to 2005-2006. That is, the average tuition, fees, room, and board at four-year private institutions have always exceeded the education benefits (figure 3) and, with few exceptions, more than 100% of the average tuition, fees, room, and board at two-year public institutions have been covered by the education benefits (figure 4).

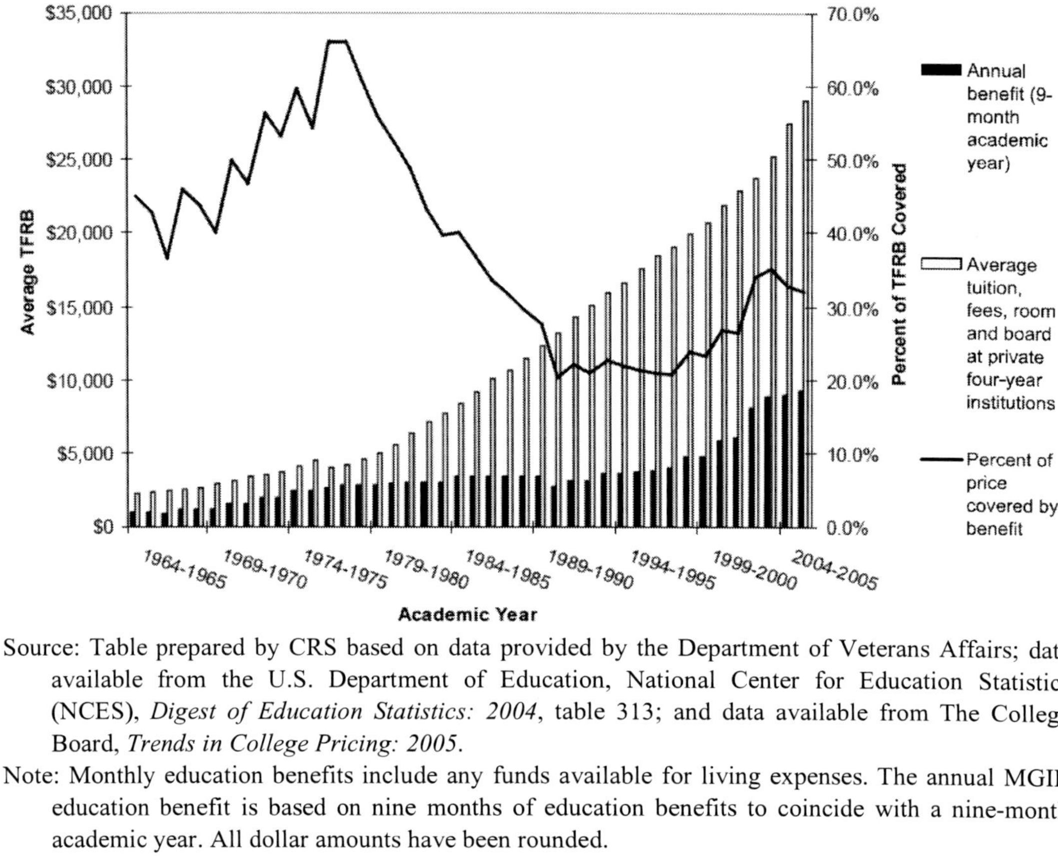

Source: Table prepared by CRS based on data provided by the Department of Veterans Affairs; data available from the U.S. Department of Education, National Center for Education Statistics (NCES), *Digest of Education Statistics: 2004*, table 313; and data available from The College Board, *Trends in College Pricing: 2005.*

Note: Monthly education benefits include any funds available for living expenses. The annual MGIB education benefit is based on nine months of education benefits to coincide with a nine-month academic year. All dollar amounts have been rounded.

Figure 3. Percentage of Average Tuition, Fees, Room and Board (TFRB) of Four-Year Private Institutions Covered by GI Bill Education Benefit: 1964-1965 through 2005-2006.

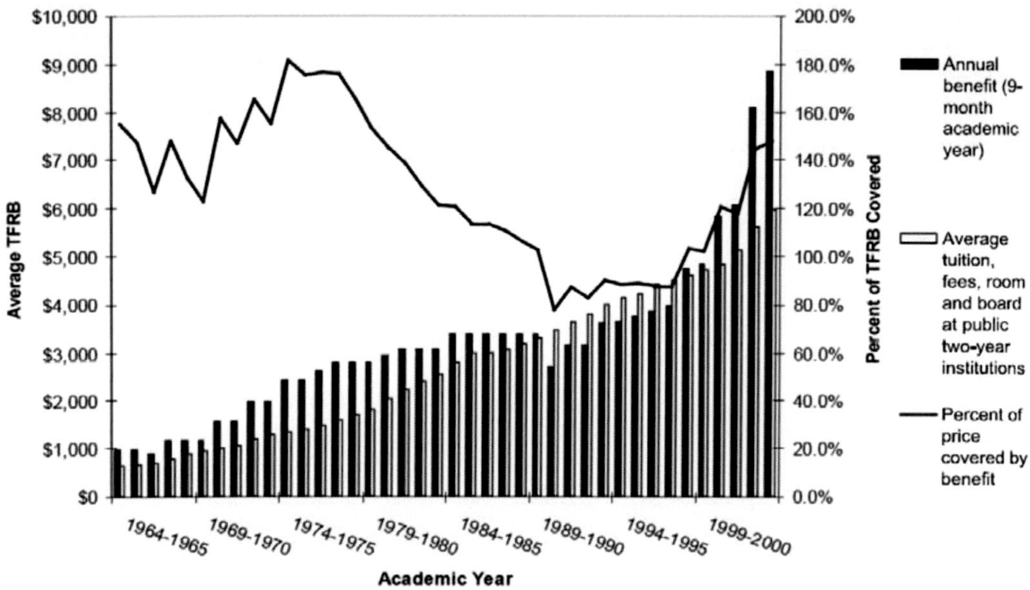

Source: Table prepared by CRS based on data provided by the Department of Veterans Affairs; data available from the U.S. Department of Education, National Center for Education Statistics (NCES), *Digest of Education Statistics: 2004*, table 313; and data available from The College Board, *Trends in College Pricing: 2005*.

Note: Monthly education benefits include any funds available for living expenses. The annual MGIB education benefit is based on nine months of education benefits to coincide with a nine-month academic year. All dollar amounts have been rounded.

Figure 4. Percent of Average Tuition, Fees, Room and Board (TFRB) of Two-Year Public Institutions Covered by GI Bill Education Benefit: 1964-1965 through 2003-2004.

POSSIBLE CHANGES TO GI EDUCATION BENEFITS WITH RESPECT TO COLLEGE PRICE

Based on figure 1, it appears that the current MGIB benefits usually have not been as generous as those provided in past years and have not covered as much of the price of attendance as previous benefits (figures 2 -4). As previously discussed, however, beginning with the Korean GI Bill, there was a sense that having beneficiaries contribute to the cost of their education was important. It should be noted that under the MGIB, program participants initially contribute to their education through payroll reductions.

If there is interest in ensuring that benefits cover the price of a specific level of education, such as the price of a four-year or two-year public institution, there are several possible steps that policymakers could take. Congress could increase or decrease the monthly benefit to a level that would equal or exceed the current price of tuition, fees, room, and board at a specific type of institution.[18] In subsequent years, benefits could be increased based on the most recent data available on college price, an average of college price over a multi-year period, or by linking increases in education benefits to changes in the Consumer Price Index-All Urban Consumers (CPI-U) for college tuition and fees.[19] Congress currently links increases in the education benefit to the overall CPI-U, while also making additional adjustments occasionally.[20] The college tuition and fees index has been increasing more rapidly than the *overall* CPI-U since 1984.[21] Therefore, linking the GI Bill education benefit to the CPI-U for tuition and fees would help to ensure that benefits are keeping pace with changes in tuition and fees at the chosen type of institution. If Congress chooses to leave current benefits at their current level, the latter option could be implemented to ensure that benefits keep pace with changes in tuition and fees.[22]

USE OF EDUCATION BENEFITS

For FY2004 (the most recent data available), of the 490,397 beneficiaries receiving benefits, more beneficiaries participated in MGIB-AD (68%) than in any other program (figure 5). The MGIB-AD also distributed the most money to beneficiaries in FY2004 — $1.8 billion out of a total of $2.4 billion (76%).

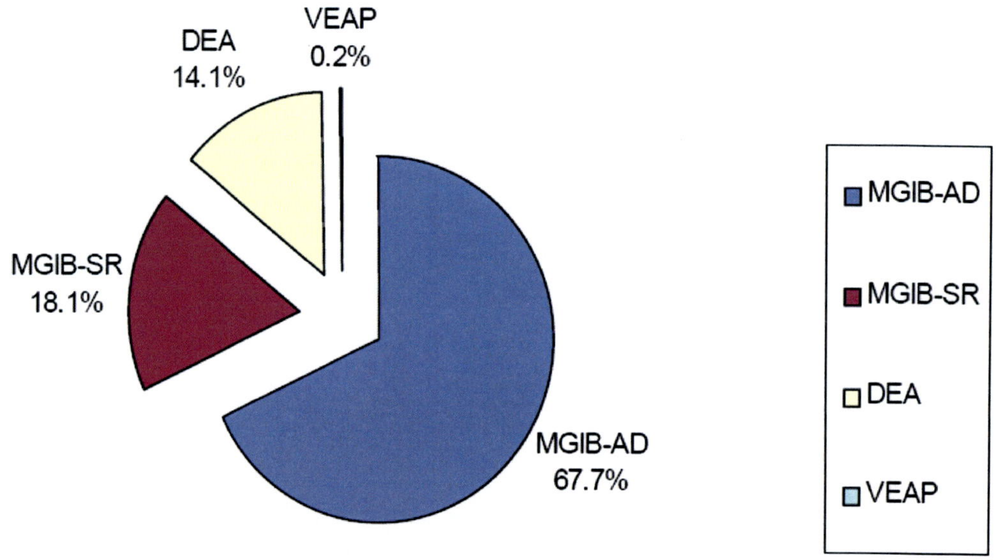

Source: Chart created by CRS based on data provided by the Department of Veterans Affairs.

Figure 5. Percentage of Education Beneficiaries by Program: FY2004.

With respect to how benefits are utilized for postsecondary education, as illustrated in figure 6, a large majority of beneficiaries across all four programs used their benefits to pursue undergraduate education. Most notably, approximately 92% of MGIB-SR and 85% of MGIB-AD beneficiaries utilized their benefits to pursue undergraduate education in FY2004.

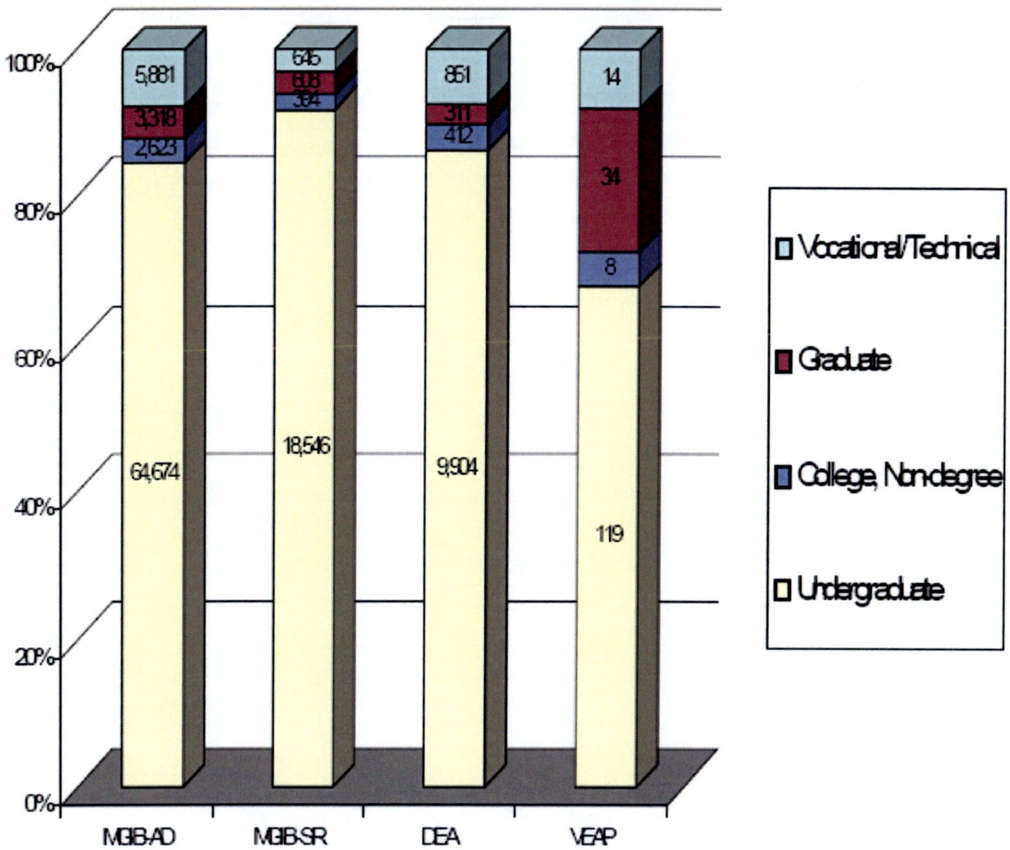

Source: Chart created by CRS based on data provided by the U.S. Department of Veterans Affairs.

Figure 6. Education and Training Pursued by Beneficiaries by Military Education Program: FY2004.

Title IV Federal Student Aid Program Descriptions

This section discusses the federal student aid programs under Title IV of the HEA and the treatment of military education benefits under these programs. It describes each of the federal student aid programs, including a general discussion of how they function and how each of the programs interacts with military education benefits. In addition, the basic structure of the federal student aid need analysis system is included to explain how military education benefits are treated.

The federal student aid programs authorized in Title IV of the HEA provide grant aid (which does not have to be repaid), loans, and work-study assistance. The largest Title IV student aid programs are federal Pell Grants and federal student loans. Under each, students receive funds to attend the eligible postsecondary education institution of their choice.[23] A brief description of each of the Title IV student aid programs follows.[24]

Federal Pell Grants

The Pell Grant program provides grants to financially needy undergraduate students. In any year, federal funding is available to ensure that all eligible students attending eligible institutions receive a Pell Grant. Pell Grants are portable; that is, the grant aid follows students to the eligible postsecondary education institution in which they enroll. The size of the grant is based, principally, on the financial resources that students and their families are expected to contribute toward postsecondary education expenses, and the appropriated maximum grant. For FY2006, the appropriated maximum grant is $4,050.[25]

Student Loans

The federal government operates two major student loan programs: the Federal Family Education Loan program (FFEL) and the William D. Ford Direct Loan program (DL). The FFEL program insures and subsidizes loans that private lenders make to students or their parents to help them meet the costs of postsecondary education. FFELs are made by private lenders and are available to undergraduate and graduate students, and their parents. Certain types of FFELs are need-based; others are not. Several types of FFEL program loans are available, including federal need-based subsidized Stafford loans (under which the government pays the interest while the borrower is in school, or during a grace period or deferment); unsubsidized Stafford loans; federal PLUS loans (for parents of undergraduate students); and federal consolidation loans. A common feature of all of these loans is that the federal government guarantees lenders against loss through borrower default, death, permanent disability, or, in limited instances, bankruptcy. Lenders are also provided an interest subsidy to insure a sufficient return given financial market conditions.

Unlike FFEL, DLs are made by the federal government to students through their institutions, thus eliminating the need for private capital and guaranty agencies.[26] Schools may serve as direct loan originators, or the loans may be originated as well as serviced by contractors working for ED. Loan terms and conditions for DLs are generally the same as those in the FFEL programs.[27]

Campus-Based Programs

Three smaller Title IV student aid programs — Federal Supplemental Educational Opportunity Grants (FSEOG), Federal Work-Study, and Federal Perkins Loans — are collectively known as the campus-based programs because their funds are allocated to postsecondary institutions for award to students. Institutions must match a portion of their allocation under each of these programs. Undergraduate students can participate in each of these programs, while graduate students are only eligible for Work-Study and Perkins Loans.[28]

Leveraging Educational Assistance Partnership

Another relatively small student aid program under Title IV is the Leveraging Educational Assistance Partnership (LEAP) program. LEAP provides matching federal funds to states to encourage and assist them in providing eligible postsecondary students with need-based grant and work-study aid.[29]

FEDERAL NEED ANALYSIS

The expected family contribution (EFC) is the amount that the federal need analysis system (Title IV, Part F) determines a family has available to contribute toward postsecondary education expenses. In calculating the EFC, consideration is given to available income (a combination of taxable and untaxed income and benefits) and, for some families, available assets. In addition, living expenses, retirement needs, and federal and state tax liability are considered. The income contribution is calculated by determining the total income of a student and his or her family (where applicable), determining available income by subtracting a series of allowances from total income, and then considering a percentage of that available income as an income contribution toward postsecondary education costs. A contribution from assets is similarly calculated. The combination of the available income contribution and asset contribution divided by the number of individuals in the family enrolled in college constitutes the EFC.

The calculation of the EFC varies depending upon the applicant's dependency status. There are three separate dependency classifications for individual applicants: dependent student, independent student with dependents, and independent student without dependents. These distinctions are important because parental financial information is *not* considered if the applicant meets the statutory definition of an *independent student*. To be classified as statutorily independent [Title IV, Section 480(d)], an applicant must meet **one** of the following conditions:

- 24 years of age or older;
- married;
- enrolled in a graduate or professional program;
- have a dependent other than a spouse;
- orphan or ward of the court (or was up until age 18); or
- a military veteran[30] or active duty service member.

Students who do not meet any of the aforementioned conditions are considered to be dependent for the purposes of Title IV student aid.

Cost of attendance (COA) is determined by each higher education institution. The COA is a measure of student's educational expenses at a specific IHE.[31] In general, it is the sum of tuition and fees; an allowance for books, supplies, transportation, and miscellaneous personal expenses; and a room and board allowance.

The financial aid administrator determines the student's need for federal aid and other sources of aid, based primarily upon the EFC and COA. This is true for all federal student aid programs except for the Pell Grant program (see below). The final outcome is the financial aid award or package, which consists of the specific sources and amounts of student aid each applicant will receive to help pay for his/her education-related expenses.[32]

Military Education Benefits and Need Analysis

This section describes military education benefits and how they are treated in the federal need analysis system. In addition, where applicable, specific Title IV programs and their relationship to military education benefits in determining the amount of aid awarded for the specific Title IV program and/or in calculating the students' need for federal student aid are also discussed.

Military education benefits[33] are not treated as income, and therefore are not utilized in calculating the EFC. However, depending upon the federal student aid program, veterans' education benefits may be treated as a *resource* or *other estimated financial assistance* (to be discussed).[34] Financial need is calculated by subtracting the EFC and resources or other estimated financial assistance from the student's COA. As a result, as the amount of the EFC or estimated financial assistance/resources increases, the amount of need declines, which reduces the amount of need-based aid a student can receive.

Military Education Benefits and Pell Grants

The primary Pell Grant award rule is that a student's annual grant is the lesser of three different amounts: the maximum appropriated Pell Grant minus EFC; COA minus EFC; or the tuition sensitivity amount.[35] For nearly all Pell recipients, the Pell Grant award is calculated by subtracting the EFC from the maximum appropriated Pell Grant for the year (i.e., without regard for the COA). This is because the maximum Pell Grant minus the recipient's EFC is almost always lower than the COA minus the EFC. Because military education benefits are not considered in calculating the EFC, the receipt of these benefits does not affect a student's Pell Grant award.

Military Education Benefits and Federal Student Loans

The amount of federal student loans awarded is primarily dependent upon a student's EFC, other estimated financial assistance, and the COA of the postsecondary institution that the student chooses to attend. As a result, as the amount of the EFC or estimated financial assistance increases, a recipient's unmet need declines, reducing eligibility for need-based student loans.

Under the provisions of the Higher Education Amendments of 1998 (P.L. 105-244), MGIB benefits, but not other veterans' education benefits,[36] are excluded from consideration as estimated financial assistance for purposes of *subsidized* Stafford Loans, but not for unsubsidized Stafford Loans. As a result, receipt of MGIB benefits does not reduce a student's financial need for subsidized Stafford Loans, but does reduce a student's financial need for unsubsidized loans.

Military Education Benefits and Campus-Based Programs

For campus-based student aid programs, military education benefits, including MGIB benefits, are considered to be a resource. As a result, veterans' education benefits, including MGIB benefits, directly affect the determination of a student's need for campus-based student aid. Program regulations, issued in 1999 by ED, permit an institution of higher education, in its determination of a student's campus-based assistance, to exclude from consideration as a resource any portion of a subsidized student loan up to the amount of a student's active duty MGIB benefits.[37] This regulatory authority has the effect of allowing an institution to protect — if it chooses to do so — a certain amount of the subsidized loan assistance from having an adverse effect on the MGIB benefit recipient's campus-based assistance.

STUDENT ELIGIBILITY REQUIREMENTS FOR TITLE IV PROGRAMS AND MILITARY EDUCATION BENEFITS

As illustrated by table 4, few similarities exist between the student eligibility requirements for Title IV programs and the eligibility requirements for military education benefits. The only similarity among all of the programs is that a student must maintain satisfactory academic progress — as determined by the institution — while enrolled.

The differences between the programs are primarily eligibility-related, and are targeted to the particular program. For example, the eligibility requirements for military education benefits generally focus on the beneficiary's time and duration of service, the amount that was contributed toward the benefit, and how much the recipient is eligible to receive. Similarly, the eligibility requirements for the Title IV programs generally relate to the student having the requisite education and citizenship status, not having a drug conviction, not owing money to the federal government, and registering for the Selective Service (where applicable).

Table 4. Student Eligibility Requirements for Participation in the Federal Student Aid Programs Under Title IV of the Higher Education Act and GI Bill Education Benefits

Eligibility criteria	HEA, Title IV programs	Montgomery GI Bill-Active Duty	Montgomery GI Bill-Selected Reserve	Veterans Education Assistance Program (VEAP)
Citizenship requirement	Generally, students must be U.S. citizens or U.S. permanent residents. Individuals with several other entrance statuses can qualify for aid	N/A	N/A	N/A
Contribution	N/A	Pay reduction of $100 per month for the first 12 months of pay	None	$25 to $100 per month; $2,700 maximum.
Discharge requirement	N/A	Fully honorable	Must remain with Reserve unit	Conditions other than dishonorable
Drug conviction	Conviction for possession or sale of drugs can disqualify students for federal student aid	N/A	N/A	N/A
Duration of benefits	N/A	Lesser of 36 months or number of months on active duty	36 months	Lesser of 36 months or number of months they contributed
Education requirement	Students must have a high school diploma or the recognized equivalent; absent such a diploma or its equivalent, students must demonstrate an ability to benefit from postsecondary education by passing an examination approved by the Department of Education	High school diploma or equivalency, or 12 hours of college credit	High school diploma or equivalency before applying for benefits	N/A
Eligibility criteria	HEA, Title IV programs	Montgomery GI Bill-Active Duty	Montgomery GI Bill-Selected Reserve	Veterans Education Assistance Program (VEAP)
Enrollment status	Must be enrolled or accepted for enrollment in a degree, certificate, or other program leading to a recognized educational credential	Courses must lead to an educational, professional, or vocational objective.	Courses must lead to an educational, professional, or vocational objective	Courses must lead to an educational, professional, or vocational objective
Imprisonment	Students who are incarcerated in a federal or state penal institution are ineligible for a Pell Grant, but may qualify for other federal aid	Only the costs of tuition and fees, necessary books, and supplies are covered	Benefits will be reduced	Only the costs of tuition and fees, necessary books, and supplies are covered

Table 4. (Continued).

Eligibility criteria	HEA, Title IV programs	Montgomery GI Bill-Active Duty	Montgomery GI Bill-Selected Reserve	Veterans Education Assistance Program (VEAP)
Length of service	N/A	Served continuously for 181 days or more; 24 months of active duty if enlisted after September 7, 1980	Accepted 6-year reserve obligation after June 30, 1985	Minimum 181 continuous days of active duty service, if entered before October 16, 1981; 24 months of continuous active duty service if entered after October 16, 1981
Money owed to federal government	Cannot owe a refund on a grant previously received, or be in default on any education loan	N/A	N/A	N/A
Period of service	N/A	Entered active duty after June 30, 1985	July 1, 1985, to present	December 31, 1976, through July 1, 1985
Eligibility criteria	HEA, Title IV programs	Montgomery GI Bill-Active Duty	Montgomery GI Bill-Selected Reserve	Veterans Education Assistance Program (VEAP)
Progress while enrolled	Students have to maintain satisfactory academic progress while enrolled in postsecondary education in order to be eligible for federal student aid; satisfactory progress is delineated by policies developed by each participating higher education institution.	Satisfactory attendance, conduct, and progress, as determined by the institution	Satisfactory attendance, conduct, and progress, as determined by the institution	Satisfactory attendance, conduct and progress, as determined by the institution
Selective Service registration	Males between ages 18-25 must register for the selective service.	N/A	N/A	N/A
Time limitation on use of benefits	N/A	Within 10 years of discharge or release from active duty	Within 14 years of initial eligibility, if eligible on or after October 1, 1992 — prior to October 1, 1992, benefits must be used within 10 years of initial eligibility	Within 10 years of discharge or release from active duty

Source: Table prepared by CRS based on data available from the U.S. Department of Education, U.S. Department of Veterans Affairs, relevant legislation, and the Code of Federal Regulations.

REFERENCES

[1] Some of the historical information about the GI Bill was adapted from CRS Report 94-221, *Veterans' Educational Assistance Programs*, byMaryF. Smith and William J. Krouse. This report is available from the authors of the current report.

[2] Reliable, comprehensive data on the price of college attendance during the 1940s are not available. Based on data obtained on individual institutions, it seems likely that $500 annually would have been sufficient to cover educational costs at most institutions. For example, based on anecdotal evidence tuition and fees at Harvard University and the Massachusetts Institute of Technology were $450 and $500, respectively, in the 1940s.

[3] In 1976, at the end of the Vietnam hostilities, benefits were extended from 36 months to 45 months, and the time period in which benefits could be used was extended from eight years to 10 years following discharge.

[4] The Department of Defense could also make additional contributions, known as "kickers," to individuals in critical military fields to encourage enlistment or reenlistment in the Armed Forces.

[5] The New GI Bill Continuation Act (P.L. 100-48) permanently authorized the All-Volunteer Force Educational Assistance Program and the Selected Reserve Component. It also changed the name of the program to the Montgomery GI Bill.

[6] This program was authorized by the Ronald W. Reagan National Defense Authorization Act for FY2005 (P.L. 108-375). Given the recent implementation of this program, this program is not discussed or examined in detail in this report.

[7] Other payment distribution arrangements are possible.

[8] This report uses data on four-year public universities and private universities prior to the 1975-1976 academic year, and data from all four-year public institutions and all four-year private institutions for subsequent years.

[9] Veterans with dependents have historically received additional funding to acknowledge this added responsibility under programs prior to VEAP.

[10] All constant dollar calculations were performed using an inflation calculator available from the U.S. Bureau of Labor Statistics (BLS). The inflation calculator uses the average Consumer Price Index-All Urban Consumers (CPI-U) for each year. The calculator is available at [http://data.bls.gov/cgi-bin/cpicalc.pl].

[11] This assumes that living expenses were provided for nine months each year, the length of a traditional academic year. P.L. 78-346 specifically refers to an "ordinary school year" when discussing education benefits. The monthly allowance for living expenses increased to $65 in 1946 and $75 in 1948.

[12] Details may not add to totals due to rounding.

[13] Benefits provided through the original GI Bill were converted to monthly amounts for comparison purposes.

[14] In 1967, the monthly benefit increased to $130.

[15] No monthly benefit is included for VEAP because benefits were based on the amount contributed. Some programs overlap because eligibility was established according to the period of service rather than the date of separation from service.

[16] The original legislation is often referred to as having the most generous provisions. This could be because the original legislation established for the first time not only education benefits for veterans but also such individual assistance as unemployment benefits; loan guarantees for a home, farm, or business; and job-finding assistance. When all these benefits are considered collectively, it may be that the 1944 bill was the most generous. With respect to the amount of money provided for education benefits (in constant dollars), the benefits provided from 1944 through 1950 were among the most generous.

[17] For both analyses, prices are based on in-state tuition and fees and room and board rates paid by full-time-equivalent students enrolled in degree-granting institutions. While GI Bill recipients may choose not to live on campus, room and board for on-campus residency were used in the calculations because these prices are comparable to or higher than room and board expenses for students living off-campus (The College Board, *Trends in College Pricing: 2004* and the College Board, *Trends in College Pricing: 2005*. Available online at [http://www.collegeboard.com].) Therefore, analyzing how much the GI Bill contributed toward tuition, fees, room, and board for students living on campus provides a good indicator of whether the benefit was generous enough to cover room and board expenses for students living off campus.

[18] The benefit could be made more generous by also accounting for the price of books, supplies, transportation, and other expenses. In addition, Congress could also base the benefit on the price of attending a public two-year institution, a private four-year institution, or the average price of attending any type of postsecondary institution. Data on these prices are available through the U.S. Department of Education and The College Board.

[19] In the long run, however, it may be difficult to set this benefit level in advance of an academic year, since the first comprehensive data on college prices for a given academic year are generally published in the fall of that academic year. Instead, the GI education benefit could be set based on the previous academic year's price of attendance. This would be fairly simple to determine using the College Board data based on a sample of institutions. Data for all postsecondary institutions collected by the National Center for Education Statistics (NCES) at the U.S. Department of Education are not as timely and would not provide data for the previous year. For example, NCES recently published preliminary price data for the 2003-2004 academic year.

[20] Benefits are increased based on the amount by which (1) the CPI-U for the 12-month period ending June 30 preceding the beginning of the fiscal year for which the increase will take effect exceeds (2) the CPI-U for the 12-month period prior to the 12-month period discussed in (1). For more information, see 38 U.S.C. 3015. For the purposes of this report, constant dollar calculations were made using the annual CPI-U index.

[21] From 1984 to 2005, the overall annual CPI-U increased from 107.6 to 195.3. During the same time period, the college tuition and fees index increased from 109.9 to 475.1, according to the U.S. Bureau of Labor Statistics.

[22] The CPI-U for college tuition and fees does not include room and board.

[23] For additional information regarding institutional eligibility requirements to participate in the Title IV student aid programs, see CRS Report RL31926, *Institutional Eligibility for Participation in Title IV Student Aid Programs Under the Higher Education Act: Background and Issues*, by Rebecca R. Skinner.

[24] Other programs to support individuals receiving military education benefits are available, such as the student work-study Allowance Program administered by the U.S. Department of Veterans Affairs. These programs are beyond the scope of this report. Additional information about these programs may be found at the U.S. Department of Veterans Affairs' website at [http://www.va.gov].

[25] For additional information about the Pell Grant program, see CRS Report RL31668, *Federal Pell Grant Program of the Higher Education Act: Background and Reauthorization*, by Charmaine Mercer.

[26] Guaranty agencies are state agencies created by state governments or private nonprofit agencies operating only within a state or nationally. Each state has a guaranty agency selected to serve as the "designated" guarantor of FFELs for students going to schools in the state or state residents going to schools elsewhere.

[27] For additional information about the federal student loan programs, see CRS Report RL30655, *Federal Student Loans: Terms and Conditions for Borrowers*, by Adam Stoll.

[28] For additional information about the federal campus-based programs, see CRS Report RL31618, *Campus-Based Student Financial Aid Programs Under the Higher Education Act*, by David P. Smole.

[29] For additional information about LEAP, see CRS Report RS21183, *Leveraging Educational Assistance Program: An Overview*, by Laura L. Monagle.

[30] Section 480(c) defines a veteran as an individual who was engaged in the active duty in the U.S. Army, Navy, Air Force, Marines or Coast Guard; and was released under a condition other than dishonorable.

[31] See HEA Title IV, Section 472 for relevant statutory language.

[32] For a more detailed description of the federal student aid need analysis system, see CRS Report RL33266, *Federal Student Aid Need Analysis System: Background, Description and Legislative Action*, by Charmaine Mercer.

[33] HEA Section 480(c)(2) defines "veterans' education benefits" as including, but not limited to, 10 different sources of veterans' education support. In addition to the Montgomery GI Bill benefits, these include benefits from such sources as the Dependents Educational Assistance program (U.S.C., Title 38, Chapter 35), and the Reserve Officer Training Corps program (U.S.C., Title 37, Chapter 2).

[34] The program regulations for the campus-based programs refer to other types of aid, such as veterans' education benefits, as a resource and the federal Stafford Loan programs refer to them as estimated financial assistance. HEA Title IV, Section 480(j)(1) states that for the purpose of determining a student's eligibility for funds under this title, *estimated financial assistance* shall include all scholarships, grants, loans, or other assistance known to the institution at the time the determination of the student's need is made, including veterans' education benefits as defined in Subsection (c), and national service education awards or post-service benefits under Title I of the National and Community Service Act of 1990. According to the *Federal Student Aid Handbook, 2004-2005*, the term *resources* comprises aid from federal student aid programs, as well as grants, scholarships, loans, and need-based employment that a financial aid administrator can reasonably anticipate at the time he/she awards aid to the student, regardless of whether the assistance is awarded by the school or by an individual or organization outside the school (pp. 3-90).

[35] As implemented by ED, tuition sensitivity reduces the Pell Grant award received by a small number of the poorest students attending institutions with very low tuition charges. For FY2005, the only students whose Pell Grant may possibly be reduced under tuition sensitivity are those students whose tuition charges (and any allowances for dependent care or disability-related expenses) are less than $675; whose EFCs are $700 or less; and whose total COA is $3,400 or higher.

[36] For example, Survivors' and Dependents' Educational Assistance (Title 38, Chapter 35) may be considered in determining estimated financial need for subsidized or unsubsidized Stafford Loans.

[37] *Federal Register*, October 28, 1999, p. 58292.

In: No Child Left Behind: Issues and Developments
Editor: P. H. Berkhart, pp. 83-101
ISBN: 978-1-60456-210-1

Chapter 4

THE ELEMENTARY AND SECONDARY EDUCATION ACT, AS AMENDED BY THE NO CHILD LEFT BEHIND ACT: A PRIMER*

Wayne C. Riddle and Rebecca R. Skinner

ABSTRACT

The primary source of federal aid to K-12 education is the Elementary and Secondary Education Act (ESEA), particularly its Title I, Part A program of Education for the Disadvantaged. The ESEA was initially enacted in 1965 (P.L. 89-10), and was most recently amended and reauthorized by the No Child Left Behind Act of 2001 (NCLBA, P.L. 107-110). Virtually all ESEA programs are authorized through FY2008. During the current 110th Congress, congressional hearings are being conducted in anticipation of subsequent consideration of legislation to amend and extend the ESEA.

The NCLBA initiated a major expansion of federal influence upon several aspects of public K-12 education, primarily with the aim of increasing the accountability of public school systems and individual public schools for improving achievement outcomes of all pupils, especially the disadvantaged. States must implement in all public schools and school districts a variety of standards-based assessments in reading, math and science; make complex annual adequate yearly progress (AYP) determinations for each public school and district; and require virtually all public school teachers and aides to meet a variety of qualification requirements. State AYP policies must incorporate an ultimate goal of all public school pupils reaching a proficient or higher level of achievement by the end of the 2013-14 school year. Further, participating states must enforce a series of increasingly substantial consequences for most of their schools and almost all school districts that fail to meet the AYP standards for two consecutive years or more. All of these requirements are associated with state participation in the ESEA Title I-A program.

Other major ESEA programs provide grants to support the education of migrant students; recruitment of and professional development for teachers; language instruction for limited English proficient students; drug abuse prevention programs; after-school instruction and care; expansion of charter schools and other forms of public school

* Excerpted from CRS Report RL33960, dated April 12, 2007.

choice; education services for Native American, Native Hawaiian, and Alaska Native students; Impact Aid to compensate local educational agencies for taxes foregone due to certain federal activities; and a wide variety of innovative educational approaches or instruction to meet particular student needs.

This report provides a brief overview of major provisions of the ESEA. It will not be updated.

INTRODUCTION

The primary source of federal aid to K-12 education is the Elementary and Secondary Education Act (ESEA), particularly its Title I, Part A program of Education for the Disadvantaged. The ESEA was initially enacted in 1965 (P.L. 89-10), and was most recently amended and reauthorized by the No Child Left Behind Act of 2001 (NCLBA, P.L. 107-110). ESEA programs are explicitly authorized through FY2007, although they were automatically extended for one additional year when Congress did not act upon reauthorization legislation by December 31, 2005.[1] Currently in the 110th Congress, congressional hearings are being conducted in anticipation of subsequent consideration of legislation to amend and extend the ESEA.

The NCLBA initiated a major expansion of federal influence on several aspects of public K-12 education, primarily with the aim of increasing the accountability of public school systems and individual public schools for improving achievement outcomes of all pupils, especially the disadvantaged. States must implement in all public schools and school districts a variety of standards-based assessments in reading, math and science; make complex annual adequate yearly progress (AYP) determinations for each public school and district; and require virtually all public school teachers and aides to meet a variety of qualification requirements. State AYP policies must incorporate an ultimate goal of all public school pupils reaching a proficient or higher level of achievement by the end of the 2013-2014 school year. Further, participating states must enforce a series of increasingly substantial consequences for most of their schools and almost all school districts that fail to meet the AYP standards for two consecutive years or more. All of these requirements are associated with state participation in the ESEA Title I-A program.

Other major ESEA programs provide grants to support the education of migrant students; recruitment of and professional development for teachers; language instruction for limited English proficient (LEP) students; drug abuse prevention programs; after-school instruction and care; expansion of charter schools and other forms of public school choice; education services for Native American, Native Hawaiian, and Alaska Native students; Impact Aid to compensate local educational agencies for taxes foregone due to certain federal activities; and a wide variety of innovative educational approaches or instruction to meet particular student needs.

This report provides a brief overview of major provisions of the ESEA. It is organized by title and part of the act. Other CRS reports provide much more detailed discussions and analyses of major ESEA provisions.[2]

TITLE I: IMPROVING THE ACADEMIC ACHIEVEMENT OF THE DISADVANTAGED

The introductory text for ESEA Title I includes the authorization of appropriations for FY2002-FY2007 for each Part of the Title, including school improvement grants, and authority for states to reserve 1% of grants under parts A, C, and D, or $400,000 (whichever is greater), for state administration.

Part A: Improving Basic Programs Operated by Local Educational Agencies

Title I, Part A, of the ESEA authorizes federal aid to local educational agencies (LEAs) for the education of disadvantaged children. Title I-A grants provide supplementary educational and related services to low-achieving and other pupils attending pre-kindergarten through grade 12 schools with relatively high concentrations of pupils from low-income families. It has also become a "vehicle" to which a number of requirements affecting broad aspects of public K-12 education for all pupils have been attached as a condition for receiving Title I-A grants.

Title I-A funds are allocated by the U.S. Department of Education (ED) to state educational agencies (SEAs), which then suballocate grants to LEAs. It is one of the few federal K-12 formula grant programs for which substate grants are, in most cases, calculated by ED. Portions of each annual appropriation for Title I-A are allocated under four different formulas — Basic, Concentration, Targeted, and Education Finance Incentive Grants — although funds allocated under all of these formulas are combined and used for the same purposes by recipient LEAs. While the allocation formulas have several distinctive elements, the primary factors used in all four formulas are estimated numbers of children aged 5-17 in poor families plus a state expenditure factor based on average expenditures per pupil for public K-12 education. Other factors included in one or more formulas include weighting schemes designed to increase aid to LEAs with the highest concentrations of poverty, and a factor to increase grants to states with high levels of expenditure equity among their LEAs. Each formula also has a LEA hold harmless provision (no LEA may receive less than 85-95% of its previous year grant, depending on the LEA's poverty rate) and a state minimum grant provision (up to either 0.25% or 0.35% of state grants, depending on the formula).

Within LEAs, Title I-A funds are used to provide supplementary educational services to pupils at public schools with the highest percentages or numbers of children from low-income families, as well as eligible pupils who live in the areas served by these public schools, but who attend private schools.[3] While there are several program rules related to school selection, the participating schools must generally have a percentage or number of children from low-income families that is greater than the LEA's average. LEAs can generally choose to focus Title I-A services on selected grade levels (e.g., only in elementary schools), but they must usually provide services in all schools, without regard to their grade level, where the percentage of pupils from low-income families is 75% or more. Once schools are selected, Title I-A funds are allocated among them on the basis of their number of pupils from low-income families.

There are two basic types of Title I-A programs. *Schoolwide programs* are authorized if the percentage of low-income pupils served by a school is 40% or higher. In schoolwide programs, Title I-A funds may be used to improve the performance of all pupils in a school. For example, funds might be used to provide professional development services to all of a school's teachers, upgrade instructional technology, or implement new curricula. The other major type of Title I-A service model is the *targeted assistance* school program. This was the original type of Title I-A program, under which Title I-A-funded services are generally limited to the lowest achieving pupils in the school. For example, pupils may be "pulled out" of their regular classroom for several hours of more intensive instruction by a specialist teacher each week, or they may receive such instruction in an after-school program, or funds may be used to hire a teacher's aide who provides additional assistance to low achieving pupils in their regular classroom. According to data for the 2002-2003 school year (the latest currently available), 54% of schools receiving Title I-A operated schoolwide programs, and these schools served 84% of all participating pupils.[4]

A number of major accountability requirements apply to public schools in a state that participates in the Title I-A program. Participating states[5] must administer annual, standards-based assessments in reading and mathematics to pupils in each of grades 3-8, plus at least once in grades 10-12. Beginning with the 2007-2008 school year, such assessments must also be administered to pupils in each of three grade levels (3-5, 6-9, and 10-12) in science. Pupil performance standards for all required assessments must establish at least three performance levels: advanced, proficient, and basic. The state assessments must meet a variety of criteria regarding accommodations for pupils with disabilities and LEP pupils, and linkages between state content standards, pupil performance standards, and assessments. Participating states must also administer annual assessments of English language proficiency to all of their LEP pupils, and participate in National Assessment of Educational Progress (NAEP) tests of 4th and 8th grade pupils in reading and math every two years.

States participating in Title I-A must use results of the required reading and math assessments to make annual adequate yearly progress (AYP) determinations. AYP standards must be applied to all public schools, LEAs, and to states overall. However, under the ESEA, consequences for failing to meet AYP standards need only be applied to schools and LEAs participating in Title I-A, and consequences for states as a whole are limited to potential identification and provision of technical assistance. AYP is defined primarily on the basis of the percentage of pupils scoring at a proficient or higher level of achievement. AYP standards must also include at least one additional academic indicator; in the case of high schools, this must be the graduation rate.

AYP calculations must be disaggregated — i.e., determined separately for several demographic groups, as well as for an "all pupils" group. The specified groups include economically disadvantaged pupils, LEP pupils, pupils with disabilities, and pupils in major racial and ethnic groups. However, pupil groups need not be considered if their number is so small that results would not be statistically significant or the identity of pupils might be divulged (minimum group size). In order to make AYP, at least 95% of pupils overall and 95% of each demographic group must participate in assessments. Schools or LEAs meet AYP standards only if they meet the required threshold levels of performance on assessments, other academic indicators, and test participation with respect to all of the designated pupil groups that meet the minimum group size criterion selected by the state. The primary structure for AYP determination under the ESEA applies the same required threshold level of achievement to all pupils and schools statewide (a "status" model). The ESEA also includes a "safe harbor" provision, under which AYP may be met by a pupil group if it experiences a 10% reduction, compared to the previous year, in the number of pupils below proficiency. In recent years, there has been increasing interest in using "growth" models to determine AYP, by which the achievement of individual pupils is tracked from year to year. Under a pilot program, a limited number of states are being allowed to use such models.

The ESEA requires states to identify LEAs and schools that fail to meet AYP standards for two consecutive years for improvement. Pupils attending these schools must be provided with options to attend other public schools that make AYP. If a Title I-A school fails to meet AYP standards for a third year, pupils from low-income families must be offered the opportunity to receive instruction from a supplemental services provider of their choice. One or more additional "corrective actions," such as implementing a new curriculum, must be taken with respect to Title I-A schools that fail to meet AYP for a fourth year. Finally, those that fail to meet AYP standards for a sixth year must implement a "restructuring" plan, involving such actions as reopening as a charter school. Procedures analogous to those for schools apply to LEAs that receive Title I-A grants and fail to meet AYP requirements.

Finally, states participating in Title I-A are required to provide that all public school teachers in core subjects are "highly qualified." In order to be deemed "highly qualified," all such public school teachers must hold at least a bachelor's degree, have obtained full state certification or passed the state teacher licensing examination, and must hold a license to teach. In addition, teachers who are new to the profession must demonstrate subject area knowledge, including (if teaching at a secondary level) passing a state academic test or completing an academic major, graduate degree, or advanced certification in each subject taught. A public school teacher who is *not* new to the profession may also be deemed to be "highly qualified" by demonstrating competence in all subjects taught "based on a high objective uniform State standard of evaluation" (HOUSSE). Further, paraprofessionals (aides) providing instruction in Title I-A programs must have either: (a) completed at least two years of higher education; or (b) earned an associate's (or higher) degree; or (c) met a "rigorous standard of quality."

Part B: Student Reading Skills Improvement Grants

Subpart 1 of Title I-B authorizes the Reading First program. Under Reading First, grants are allocated among participating states in proportion to their estimated number of children aged 5-17 in poor families, with each state receiving at least 0.25% of the total funds available for state grants. SEAs then make competitive subgrants to LEAs, with priority given to LEAs in which the estimated number of children aged 5-17 in poor families is at least 6,500 or the poverty rate for 5-17 year-olds is at least 15%. LEAs are to use these funds to improve reading programs for pupils in grades K-3 in schools that either have percentages of pupils from low-income families that are among the highest in the LEA or have been identified for improvement under Title I-A. The supported reading instruction must be grounded in scientifically based reading research. Subpart 1 also authorizes targeted assistance performance awards to states that have demonstrated improvements in pupil reading performance.

The Early Reading First program is authorized under *Subpart 2* of Title I-B. Early Reading First provides competitive grants to LEAs and/or programs serving preschool children for activities, grounded in scientifically based reading research, that are intended to help preschool children acquire knowledge and skills necessary for learning to read.

Subpart 3 of Title I-B authorizes the William F. Goodling Even Start Family Literacy Programs. Under Even Start, funds are allocated to states in proportion to grants under Title I-A, with a minimum state grant amount of the greater of $250,000 or 0.5% of total funding for state grants. Within states, funds are competitively awarded to partnerships of LEAs and other entities to provide a combination of services to parents and children, from birth to age 7, including early childhood education, adult basic education, and parenting skills training to parents lacking a high school diploma.

Subpart 4 of Title I-B authorizes grants to LEAs to improve the services provided by school libraries. If annual appropriations are less than $100 million (as has been the case each year thus far), competitive grants to LEAs are made directly by ED; if appropriations were $100 million or above, grants would be made by formula to SEAs, in proportion to Title I-A grants, and SEAs would make competitive grants to LEAs.

Part C: Education of Migratory Children

Title I-C authorizes grants to SEAs for the education of migratory children and youth. Funds are allocated by formula on the basis of each state's number of migratory children and youth aged 3-21 and the Title I-A state expenditure factor. ED may also make grants for the coordination of services and transfer of educational records for migratory students.

Part D: Prevention and Intervention Programs for Children and Youth Who Are Neglected, Delinquent, or At-Risk

Title I-D authorizes a pair of programs intended to improve education for pupils who are neglected, delinquent, or at risk of dropping out of school. *Subpart 1* authorizes grants for the education of children and youth in *state* institutions for the neglected or delinquent, including community day programs and adult correctional institutions. Funds are allocated to states on the basis of the number of such children and youth plus the Title I-A state expenditure factor. A portion of each state's grant is to be used for transition services to children and youth transferring to regular public schools. *Subpart 2* provides aid for programs operated by LEAs in collaboration with *locally operated* correctional facilities, and in coordination with the Title I-A program.

Part E: National Assessment of Title I

Title I-E requires ED to conduct a national assessment of Title I programs, including a national longitudinal study of schools participating in Title I-A and an evaluation of assessments used to meet the accountability requirements of Title I-A. Part E also authorizes grants for the demonstration of innovative practices in serving pupils assisted under Title I programs, and grants to the Close-Up Foundation of Washington, DC, for civic education programs.

Part F: Comprehensive School Reform

Title I-F authorizes grants via SEAs to LEAs to implement comprehensive reform strategies in schools participating in Title I-A. With the exception of an information and technical assistance clearinghouse, this program is not currently funded.

Part G: Advanced Placement Programs

Title I-G authorizes grants to SEAs to pay advanced placement test fees on behalf of low-income individuals, as well as grants to SEAs, LEAs, or nonprofit educational entities with relevant expertise, to support activities intended to expand access to advanced placement programs for low-income individuals.

Part H: School Dropout Prevention

At annual appropriations levels of $75 million or less (as has been the case each year thus far), Title I-H authorizes competitive grants to SEAs or LEAs for dropout prevention and reentry programs in high schools with dropout rates above the state average plus middle schools whose graduates attend these high schools. At annual appropriations levels above $75 million but less than $250 million, competitive grants would be made to SEAs for dropout prevention and reentry services to be provided via competitive subgrants to LEAs. If annual appropriations were $250 million or above, grants would be made by formula (in proportion to Title I-A grants) to SEAs, with competitive subgrants to LEAs. At all funding levels, the Secretary of Education is authorized to carry out a variety of activities as part of a "coordinated national strategy" for dropout prevention and reentry.

Part I: General Provisions

Title I-I provides for the development of federal regulations for Title I programs, state administration of these programs, and a selected number of LEA Title I-A audits. Part I also prohibits federal control of the "specific instructional content, academic achievement standards and assessments, curriculum or program of instruction" of states, LEAs, or schools (Sec. 1905), and states that nothing in Title I is to be "construed to mandate equalized spending per pupil for a State, local educational agency, or school" (Sec. 1906).

TITLE II: PREPARING, TRAINING, AND RECRUITING HIGH-QUALITY TEACHERS AND PRINCIPALS

Part A: Teacher and Principal Training and Recruiting Fund

Subpart 1 authorizes a program of state grants that may be used for a variety of purposes related to recruitment, retention, and professional development of K-12 teachers and principals. In the allocation of funds, each state first receives an amount equal to its FY2001 grant under two antecedent programs (the Eisenhower Professional Development and the Class Size Reduction programs), and remaining funds, if any, are allocated as follows: 35% on the basis of total population aged 5-17, and 65% on the basis of population aged 5-17 in poor families, with a state minimum grant amount of 0.5% of funds available for state grants. SEAs may reserve a share of funds for administration and statewide services, such as teacher or principal support programs or certification reform, and must suballocate at least 95% of grants to LEAs under *Subpart 2*. In making grants to LEAs under Subpart 2, each LEA first receives an amount equal to its FY2001 grant under the two antecedent programs noted above, and remaining funds, if any, are allocated as follows: 20% on the basis of total population aged 5-17, and 80% on the basis of population aged 5-17 in poor families. LEAs may use these grants for purposes that include recruiting and retaining highly qualified teachers, and professional development activities for teachers and principals, consistent with a locally developed needs assessment.

Subpart 3 authorizes grants to partnerships for sustained, high quality professional development services for teachers, principals, and paraprofessionals. Eligible partnerships must include an institution of higher education (IHE) with a teacher or principal education department, a school of arts and sciences within an IHE, a high-need LEA (defined as an LEA with either a school-age child poverty rate of 20% or with 10,000 school-age children in poor families, and a high percentage of teachers who are not fully certified or who are not teaching in fields or grade levels for which they were trained), and possibly additional organizations. Additional provisions of Part A authorize national activities, such as support for principal recruitment, advanced certification, and early childhood educator professional development programs, plus a National Panel on Teacher Mobility.

Part B: Mathematics and Science Partnerships

Part B authorizes grants to eligible partnerships — that include an SEA (if annual appropriations are $100 million or above), an engineering, mathematics, or science department of an IHE, and a high-need LEA (as defined in Part A) — for activities that include professional development, summer workshops or institutes, and recruitment of mathematics and science teachers, as well as development of rigorous curricula in these fields.

Part C: Innovation for Teacher Quality

Subpart 1 authorizes a pair of programs designed to encourage former members of the armed services to become teachers (Troops to Teachers), and to support alternative certification programs for mid-career professionals and others to become teachers through non-standard routes, especially in high-need LEAs (as defined in Part A) or schools (Transition to Teachers). *Subpart 2* authorizes grants to a nonprofit organization, the National Writing Project, which, through a series of contracts with IHEs and other nonprofit entities, provides professional development training to teachers of writing. *Subpart 3* authorizes a pair of grants to nonprofit organizations, the Center for Civic Education and the National Council on Economic Education, as well as other organizations experienced in the development of civic and economic educational materials for use in the schools of other nations. These grants are used to support civic education in U.S. schools, plus civic and economic educational exchange programs between the United States and Central or Eastern European nations, Ireland, or any developing country. *Subpart 4* authorizes the Teaching of Traditional American History program, under which competitive grants are made for instructional improvement to partnerships that include an IHE, a nonprofit history or humanities organization, and a library or museum. *Subpart 5* sets limits on the liability of teachers for actions taken to maintain classroom discipline; it applies to states that receive funds under any ESEA program.

Part D: Enhancing Education through Technology

Subpart 1 of Part D authorizes grants to SEAs and LEAs to increase access to educational technology, support the integration of technology into instruction, enhance technological literacy, and support technology-related professional development of teachers. Funds are allocated to states in proportion to Title I-A grants, with a state minimum grant amount of 0.5% of total funding for state grants. At least 95% of state grants must be allocated to LEAs (and consortia of LEAs and other entities) — 50% by formula, in proportion to Title I-A grants, and 50% competitively. *Subpart 2* authorizes support for national activities related to educational technology, including development of a national long range technology plan. *Subpart 3* authorizes the Ready-to-Learn Television program, under which support is provided to one or more public telecommunications entities to support the production and distribution of educational programs for preschool and elementary school pupils and their parents to support school readiness and student academic achievement. *Subpart 4* requires LEAs or schools receiving aid under Part D to establish and implement Internet safety policies designed to prevent minors from accessing material that is obscene, includes child pornography, or is harmful to minors, and prevent adults from accessing material that is obscene or includes child pornography.

Title III: Language Instruction for Limited English Proficient and Immigrant Students

Title III of the ESEA authorizes funds to support the education of LEP and immigrant students. For fiscal years in which appropriations equal or exceed $650 million, Title III, Part A, the English Language Acquisition, Language Enhancement, and Academic Achievement Act, is in effect. If appropriations are less than $650 million, Title III, Part B, Improving Language Instruction Educational Programs, is in effect. Since FY2002, appropriations have exceeded $650 million, meaning only Title III, Part A has been in effect. Therefore, only Part A is discussed below.

Part A: English Language Acquisition, Language Enhancement, and Academic Achievement Act

Title III-A was designed to help ensure that LEP students, including immigrant students, attain English proficiency, develop high levels of academic attainment in English, and meet the same state academic content and student academic achievement standards that all students are expected to meet. Formula grant allocations are made to states based on the proportion of LEP students and immigrant students in each state relative to all states. These amounts are weighted by 80% and 20%, respectively, resulting in a formula allocation based primarily on the number of LEP students in each state. States make subgrants to eligible entities (often LEAs) based on the relative number of LEP students in schools served by the eligible entity. States are also required to reserve up to 15% of the state allocation to make grants to eligible entities that have experienced a significant increase in the number of immigrant students enrolled in schools in the geographic area served by the eligible entity.

Eligible entities receiving subgrants are required to use funds for two activities. Funds must be used to increase the English language proficiency of LEP students by providing high-quality instructional programs that are grounded in scientifically based research that demonstrates the program is effective in increasing English language proficiency and student academic achievement in core academic subjects.

Funds must also be used to provide high-quality professional development to school staff or community-based personnel that work with LEP students. Eligible entities receiving grants from the funds reserved specifically for immigrant students are required to use these funds to support activities that "provide enhanced instructional opportunities" for immigrant students.

Each SEA is required to develop and hold eligible entities responsible for meeting annual measurable achievement objectives (AMAOs) for LEP students. AMAOs must include objectives for the following measures:

- Annual increases in the number or percentage of students making progress in attaining English proficiency;
- Annual increases in the number or percentage of students attaining English proficiency by the end of each school year; and
- AYP targets for LEP students on annual assessments (under Title IA).

While Title III-A focuses on the education of LEP students, Title I-A also contains provisions that specifically apply to this student population. For example, Title I-A requires that LEAs annually assess the English proficiency of all students with limited English proficiency (Section 1111(b)(7)). These assessments must measure students' speaking, listening, reading, and writing skills in English.

National Programs (Sections 3131 and 3303)

In the reservations of funds made under Title III-A, funds are provided to support two specific national programs: (1) the National Professional Development Project; and (2) the National Clearinghouse. Under the National Professional Development Project, grants are awarded on a competitive basis for a period of up to five years to IHEs working in consortia with SEAs or LEAs to provide for professional development activities that will improve classroom instruction for LEP students and to help personnel working with these students to meet professional standards (e.g., licensure, certification). The National Clearinghouse is responsible for collecting, analyzing, synthesizing, and disseminating information about language instruction educational programs for LEP students and related programs.

TITLE IV: 21ST CENTURY SCHOOLS

Title IV of the ESEA authorizes the Safe and Drug-Free Schools and Communities program (Part A) and the 21st Century Community Learning Centers (Part B). It also includes requirements related to the provision of services for children in smoke-free environments (Part C).

Part A: Safe and Drug-Free Schools and Communities

Title IV-A is the federal government's major initiative to prevent drug abuse and violence in and around schools. One-half of state grant funds is allocated on the basis of total population aged 5-17, and one-half is allocated in proportion to Title I-A concentration grants, with a minimum grant amount of the greater of 0.5% of total funding for state grants or each state's grant for FY2001. SEAs subsequently make formula grants to LEAs based on each LEA's share of total Title I-A funding (60%) and share of enrollment in public and private nonprofit elementary and secondary schools (40%). Title IV-A also provides funds to state governors to create programs to deter youth from using drugs and committing violent acts in schools. National programs supporting a variety of national leadership projects designed to prevent drug abuse and violence in elementary and secondary schools (e.g., the Safe Schools/Healthy Students initiative) are also funded under Title IV-A.

Part B: 21st Century Community Learning Centers

Title IV-B supports activities provided during non-school hours that offer learning opportunities for school-aged children. Formula grants are made to states based on the proportion of Title I-A funds received by each state relative to the total amount of funding provided through Title I-A. States subsequently award grants to local entities (e.g., LEAs, community-based organizations) on a competitive basis for a period of three to five years. SEAs are required, to the extent possible, to distribute funds equitably among the various geographic areas within the state, including urban and rural communities. Eligible entities are to serve primarily students who attend schools eligible for schoolwide programs under Title I-A and the families of these students. Eligible entities may use funds for before- and after-school activities that advance student academic achievement. The program's focus, however, is currently on providing after-school activities for children and youth, and literacy-related activities for their families.

Part C: Environmental Tobacco Smoke

Title IV-C prohibits smoking in facilities providing elementary or secondary education or library services to children, if the services are funded directly or indirectly by the federal government, or the facility is constructed, operated, or maintained using federal funds.

Title V: Promoting Informed Parental Choice and Innovative Programs

Part A: Innovative Programs

Part A authorizes the Innovative Programs block grant program, under which aid is provided to SEAs and LEAs that can be used for an especially wide range of educational services and activities. Part A grants are allocated to states on the basis of total population aged 5-17, with a state minimum grant amount of 0.5% of total funding for state grants. At least 85% of Title V-A funds must be allocated by SEAs to LEAs on the basis of state-developed formulas that take into consideration each LEA's enrollment of pupils in public and private schools, with adjustments to provide increased grants per pupil to LEAs with the greatest numbers or percentages of "high cost" pupils, including those from economically disadvantaged families and those living in sparsely populated areas or areas of concentrated poverty.

Of the Part A funds that may be retained by states, no more than 15% may be used for administrative costs; remaining funds reserved by states are to be used for one or more of seven specified types of programs and services, including the broad categories of statewide education reform, school improvement programs and technical assistance activities. LEAs may use their Part A funds for any of 27 different types of "innovative assistance programs." While several of these are relatively specific (e.g., programs to provide same gender schools and classrooms), others are more general (e.g., promising education reform projects).

Part B: Public Charter Schools

Subpart 1 authorizes grants to SEAs or, if a state's SEA chooses not to participate, charter school developers, to support the development and initial implementation of public charter schools. Priority in awarding grants is to be given to states with charter school policies meeting such criteria as holding charter schools accountable for meeting clear and measurable objectives, or establishing one or more public chartering agencies that are not LEAs. Up to 5% of program funds may be reserved by ED for technical assistance to, plus studies of, charter schools. Subpart 1 also includes general provisions for allocations to charter schools under ESEA and other federal formula grant programs. *Subpart 2* authorizes ED to make grants to three or more entities to demonstrate innovative ways to help charter schools acquire appropriate facilities. *Subpart 3* authorizes competitive grants to SEAs, LEAs, or partnerships of these entities with nonprofit organizations for programs to expand public school options for K-12 students.

Part C: Magnet Schools Assistance

Part C provides grants to plan and operate magnet schools — public schools of choice designed to encourage voluntary enrollment by students of different racial backgrounds.

Part D: Fund for the Improvement of Education

Part D authorizes a series of competitive grant programs intended to support a variety of innovative K-12 educational activities. It includes both a broad authority for innovative activities selected at the discretion of the Secretary of Education, and a series of required studies (on unhealthy public school buildings, exposure of children to violent entertainment, and sexual abuse in schools), in *Subpart 1*, and a number of specific activities in *Subparts 2-21*. The availability of funds for any of these subparts, and the level of actual discretion for the Secretary, within a single appropriations authorization for all of Part D, is determined through annual appropriations legislation.

The specific programs authorized in *Subparts 2-21* of Part D include Elementary and Secondary School Counseling Programs; Partnerships in Character Education; Smaller Learning Communities; Gifted and Talented Students; Star Schools Program; Ready to Teach; Foreign Language Assistance Program; Physical Education; Community Technology Centers; Educational, Cultural, Apprenticeship, and Exchange Programs for Alaska Natives, Native Hawaiians, and Their Historical Whaling and Trading Partners in Massachusetts; Excellence in Economic Education; Grants to Improve the Mental Health of Children; Arts in Education; Parental Assistance and Local Family Information Centers; Combating Domestic Violence; Healthy, High-Performance Schools; Grants for Capital Expenses of Providing Equitable Services for Private School Students; Additional Assistance for Certain Local Educational Agencies Impacted by Federal Property Acquisition; and the Women's Educational Equity Act.

TITLE VI: FLEXIBILITY AND ACCOUNTABILITY

Part A: Improving Academic Achievement

Subpart 1 of Part A authorizes grants to states for the development and enhancement of assessments meeting the requirements of Title I-A. In the allocation of funds, each state first receives $3 million per year, and remaining funds, if any, are allocated in proportion to population aged 5-17.

Subpart 2 of Part A allows most *LEAs* to transfer up to 50% of their formula grants among selected ESEA programs, and to transfer funds from these programs *into*, but *no funds out of*, Title I-A. *States* may transfer up to 50% of the funds under the selected ESEA programs over which they have authority, except for administrative funds, among a number of ESEA programs. States may also transfer these funds into, but not out of, Title I-A.

Subpart 3 of Part A authorizes a pair of regulatory flexibility programs, State-Flex and Local-Flex. Under State-Flex, up to seven states may consolidate all of their state administration and state activity funds under a number of ESEA programs and use these funds for any purpose authorized under any ESEA program. Under a companion Local-Flex authority, a limited number of LEAs may consolidate all of their funds under a number of ESEA programs, and use these funds for any purpose authorized under any ESEA program. Under both the state and local flexibility demonstration programs, a limited number of specified types of requirements —including those regarding civil rights, fiscal accountability (particularly the requirement that funds be used only to supplement, and not supplant, non-federal funds), and equitable participation by private school pupils and teachers — may *not* be waived.

Subpart 4 of Part A requires the Secretary of Education to review whether participating states overall (i.e., not individual LEAs or schools) meet the adequate yearly progress requirements of Title I-A and the annual measurable achievement objectives of Title III-A. The Secretary is to provide technical assistance to states that fail to meet either of these requirements for 2 consecutive years, and to submit reports to Congress listing such states.

Part B: Rural Education Initiative

Subpart 1 of Part B authorizes the Small, Rural School Achievement Program (SRSA), that provides flexibility in the use of funds under several ESEA programs to rural LEAs with fewer than 600 pupils (or meeting certain other criteria). Eligible LEAs may also receive additional grants, although these are offset by amounts received under certain ESEA programs. *Subpart 2* authorizes the Rural and Low-Income School Program (RLIS), under which grants are made to rural LEAs that do not receive grants under the SRSA program and that have a school-age child poverty rate of 20% or more. The RLIS grants may be used for a variety of ESEA-related purposes.

Part C: General Provisions

Part C contains one of several prohibitions against federal control of educational curriculum, standards, and assessments (others may be found in Title I-I and Title IX-E of the ESEA, as well as other statutes). Title VI-C also contains a number of provisions regarding the National Assessment of Educational Progress that were primarily designed to support the NAEP participation requirements under Title I-A.

TITLE VII: INDIAN, NATIVE HAWAIIAN, AND ALASKA NATIVE EDUCATION

Part A: Indian Education

Subpart 1 of Part A authorizes grants to LEAs and to schools operated or funded by the Bureau of Indian Affairs (BIA). Eligible LEAs must meet Indian pupil enrollment thresholds of at least 10 pupils or 25% of total enrollment (the thresholds do not apply if the LEA is located in Alaska, California, or Oklahoma, or on or near an Indian reservation). Formula grants are allocated on the basis of the number of Indian pupils and the greater of the average expenditure per pupil for the state or 80% of the national average. The formula grants may be consolidated with grants under other federal education programs serving Indian pupils (under a demonstration project authority); and may be used for comprehensive programs of educational services for Indian pupils, such as culturally related activities and curriculum content, substance abuse prevention, and family literacy programs. *Subpart 2* of Part A authorizes competitive grants to SEAs, LEAs, Indian tribes and organizations, BIA operated or supported schools, Indian institutions (such as IHEs), or consortia of these entities for such activities as early childhood education and teacher professional development. *Subpart 3* authorizes a variety of national activities intended to improve education for Indian students, such as research, postsecondary education fellowships, programs for gifted and talented Indian pupils, adult education programs, and education planning and administration grants to Indian tribes. *Subpart 4* establishes the National Advisory Council on Indian Education, and authorizes a preference for Indian applicants under Part A grant programs.

Part B: Native Hawaiian Education

Part B authorizes a consolidated program of competitive grants to Native Hawaiian educational or community-based organizations, or other public or private nonprofit organizations with experience in operating Native Hawaiian programs, or consortia of these entities to provide a wide variety of services intended to improve education for Native Hawaiians. In the awarding of grants, priority is to be given to activities that are intended to: improve reading skills for Native Hawaiian pupils in grades K-3; meet the needs of at-risk children and youth; increase participation by Native Hawaiians in fields or disciplines in which they are underemployed; or increase the use of the Hawaiian language in instruction. Specifically authorized activities include early childhood education and care, postsecondary education scholarships, and services for Native Hawaiian students with disabilities. Title VII-B establishes a Native Hawaiian Education Council, and supports the establishment of individual island councils.

Part C: Alaska Native Education

Part C authorizes competitive grants for a variety of activities and services intended to improve education for Alaska Natives. Eligible grantees include Alaska Native organizations, entities with experience operating Alaska Native programs or instruction in Alaska Native languages, or other organizations, including SEAs and LEAs, in consortia with Alaska Native organizations. Priority is to be given to applicants that include Alaska Native regional nonprofit organizations. Authorized uses of grants include the development of curriculum materials that address the special needs of Alaska Native students, family literacy services, support for Alaska Native students in teacher preparation programs, home instruction programs, and cultural education and exchange programs.

TITLE VIII: IMPACT AID

Title VIII of the ESEA, Impact Aid, compensates LEAs for "substantial and continuing financial burden" resulting from federal activities. These activities include federal ownership of certain lands, as well as the enrollments in LEAs of children of parents who work and/or live on federal land (e.g., children of parents in the military and children living on Indian lands). The federal government provides compensation because these activities deprive LEAs of the ability to collect property or other taxes from these individuals (e.g., members of the Armed Forces living on military bases) even though the LEAs are obligated to provide free public education to their children. Thus, Impact Aid is intended to compensate LEAs for the resulting loss of tax revenue.

Title VIII authorizes several types of Impact Aid payments. These include payments under Section 8002, Section 8003, Section 8007, and Section 8008.[6] Each of these types of payments is discussed briefly below.

Section 8002. Section 8002 compensates LEAs for the federal ownership of certain property. To qualify for compensation, the federal government must have acquired the property, in general, after 1938, and the assessed value of the land at the time it was acquired must have represented at least 10% of the assessed value of all real property within an LEA's area of service.

Section 8003. Section 8003 compensates LEAs for enrolling "federally connected" children. These are children who reside with a parent who is a member of the Armed Forces living on or off federal property; reside with a parent who is an accredited foreign military officer living on or off federal property; reside on Indian lands; reside in low-rent public housing; or reside with a parent who is a civilian working and/or living on federal land.

Two payments are made under Section 8003. Section 8003(b) authorizes "basic support payments" for federally connected children. Basic support payments are allocated directly to LEAs by ED based on a formula that uses weights assigned to different categories of federally connected children and cost factors to determine maximum payment amounts. Section 8003(d) authorizes additional payments to LEAs based on the number of certain children with disabilities who are eligible to receive services under the Individuals with Disabilities Education Act (IDEA). Payments are limited to certain IDEA-eligible children, most notably those whose parents are members of the Armed Forces (residing on or off military bases), and those residing on Indian lands. Section 8003 payments account for more than 90% of total Impact Aid appropriations.

Section 8007. Section 8007 provides funds for construction and facilities upgrading to certain LEAs with high percentages of children living on Indian lands or children of military parents. These funds are used to make formula and competitive grants.

Section 8008. Section 8008 provides funds for emergency repairs and comprehensive capital improvements to 33 schools that ED owns but LEAs use to serve federally connected children. Two of the schools are located on closed military bases, and 31 facilities are operated by LEAs. Statutory language requires ED to transfer ownership of these facilities to LEAs or other entities.

Title IX: General Provisions

Part A: Definitions

Part A provides definitions of a variety of terms used frequently throughout the ESEA, such as "local educational agency," "state educational agency," "highly qualified teacher," "limited English proficient," "professional development," "scientifically based research," and "state."

Part B: Flexibility in the Use of Administrative and Other Funds

Part B authorizes SEAs and LEAs to consolidate and jointly use funds available for administration under multiple ESEA programs. In order to qualify for this flexibility, SEAs must demonstrate that a majority of their resources are provided from non-federal sources.

Part C: Coordination of Programs; Consolidated State and Local Plans and Applications

Part C authorizes SEAs and LEAs to prepare single, consolidated plans and reports for all "covered" ESEA programs (in general, these are the formula grant programs administered via SEAs).

Part D: Waivers

Under this provision, the Secretary of Education is authorized to waive most requirements associated with any program authorized by the ESEA, if specifically requested by SEAs, LEAs, Indian tribes or schools (via their LEAs).

Part E: Uniform Provisions

Subpart 1 of Part E contains provisions for the participation of private school pupils and staff in those ESEA programs where such participation is authorized.[7] Under the relevant ESEA programs, services provided to private school pupils or staff are to be equitable in relation to the number of such pupils or staff eligible for each program; are to be secular, neutral and nonideological, with no funds to be used for religious worship or instruction; and are to be developed through consultation between public and private school officials. Provision is made for bypassing SEAs and LEAs that cannot or have not provided equitable services to private school pupils or staff, and serving private school pupils and staff in these areas through neutral, third-party organizations. Provision is also made for the submission of complaints regarding implementation of these requirements. Subpart 1 also prohibits federal control of private or home schools, or the application of any ESEA requirement to any private or home school whose pupils and staff do not receive services under any ESEA program.

Subpart 2 of Part E contains a general definition of "maintenance of effort," as applied in several ESEA programs; requires ED to publish guidance on prayer in public schools, and requires LEAs receiving ESEA funds to certify to their SEAs that they do not limit the exercise of "constitutionally protected prayer" in public schools; requires recipient SEAs, LEAs, and public schools that have a "designated open forum" to provide equal access to the Boy Scouts; prohibits the use of ESEA funds to "promote or encourage sexual activity;" prohibits federal control of educational curriculum, content or achievement standards, building standards, or allocation of resources; prohibits federally sponsored testing of pupils or teachers; and requires LEAs receiving funds under any ED program to provide to the armed services access to directory information on secondary school students, unless students or their parents request that such information not be released (this provision does not apply to certain religiously affiliated private schools). Finally, under an "Unsafe School Choice Option," pupils in states receiving ESEA funds who attend a "persistently dangerous" public school, or who are victims of violent crime at school, are to be offered the opportunity to transfer to a safe public school.

Part F: Evaluations

Part F authorizes ED to reserve 0.5% of the funds appropriated for ESEA programs, other than Titles I and III, for program evaluations, if funds for this purpose are not separately authorized.

REFERENCES

[1] The General Education Provisions Act (GEPA) provides that "The authorization of appropriations for, or duration of, an applicable program shall be automatically extended for one additional fiscal year unless Congress, in the regular session that ends prior to the beginning of the terminal fiscal year of such authorization or duration, has passed legislation that becomes law and extends or repeals the authorization of such program." (20 USC 1226a)

[2] For a current listing of these reports, see [http://apps.crs.gov/cli/cli.aspx?PRDS_CLI_ITEM_ID=2487 and from=3 and fromId=5].

[3] While Title I-A funds are used to serve eligible private school pupils, funds remain under the control of public school authorities — i.e., they are not transferred to private schools.

[4] U.S. Department of Education. Office of Planning, Evaluation and Policy Development and Office of Elementary and Secondary Education. *State ESEA Title I Participation Information for 2002-03.*

[5] Currently, all states participate in ESEA Title I-A.

[6] Other significant Impact Aid provisions include Section 8004, which details policies regarding children residing on Indian lands, and Section 8009, which prohibits states from considering Impact Aid payments in determining state aid to LEAs, unless the state has an approved program to equalize expenditures among LEAs.

[7] Several ESEA programs have relatively brief private school pupil or staff participation provisions that refer to Title IX-E for details, and there are separate, detailed private school participation provisions in Titles I-A and V-A.

In: No Child Left Behind: Issues and Developments
Editor: P. H. Berkhart, pp. 103-119
ISBN: 978-1-60456-210-1

Chapter 5

A HIGHLY QUALIFIED TEACHER IN EVERY CLASSROOM: IMPLEMENTATION OF THE NO CHILD LEFT BEHIND ACT*

Jeffrey J. Kuenzi

ABSTRACT

One of the major goals of the No Child Left Behind Act of 2001 (NCLB) is to raise the achievement of students who currently fail to meet grade-level proficiency standards. Since student achievement is believed by many to depend in large part on effective teaching, the law also contains provisions designed to improve teacher quality. These provisions establish minimum teacher quality requirements and charge states and school districts with developing plans to meet them. These plans are to ensure that all schools have a *highly qualified teacher* in every classroom by the end of the 2005-2006 school year.

To be deemed *highly qualified*, NCLB requires that teachers possess a baccalaureate degree and a state teaching certificate, and that teachers also demonstrate subject-matter knowledge for their teaching level. Elementary school teachers must show knowledge of basic elementary school curricular areas. Middle and secondary school teachers must demonstrate a high level of competency in all subject areas taught. Demonstration of subject-matter knowledge and competency may be shown by passing a state certification exam or licensing test in the relevant subject(s).

This report examines implementation of NCLB requirement and estimates the extent to which schools will achieve the goal of placing a highly qualified teacher in every classroom. After describing the highly qualified teacher requirement in detail, the report analyzes data from a national survey of schools that provide information on teacher qualifications and subjects taught. These data suggest that more than four out of five teachers would have met NCLB definition of a highly qualified teacher prior to the date of enactment.

The analysis also reveals differences between highly qualified and underqualified teachers — both in terms of the teachers' characteristics and the characteristics of the schools in which they teach. The findings have important implications for future policy-

* Excerpted from CRS Report RL33333, dated August 10, 2007.

making in the area of teacher quality. The report concludes with a discussion of issues that may be considered as the Elementary and Secondary Education Act reauthorization process unfolds.

These provisions, along with the rest of the Elementary and Secondary Education Act, will likely be considered for reauthorization by the 110th Congress

It is widely believed that good teachers are critical to student learning. A large body of academic research has produced strong evidence that teacher quality is positively related to student performance. However, the strength of this research finding depends on the measure used to indicate "quality." Studies that use credentials such as degree attainment or teacher certification show weaker impacts on student performance than studies that use direct measures of teachers' pedagogical and subject-matter knowledge.[1] Nevertheless, credentials are more readily available to local school administrators that hire teachers and more easily incorporated into state and federal policy. In recent years, education policy governing the attainment of teaching credentials has evolved to incorporate pedagogy and subject expertise. General state certification exams have been replaced or enhanced with testing for knowledge of subject matter. Some states have developed multi-tiered, knowledge-based certification systems. Teacher preparation programs in some states have begun requiring that candidates obtain a major or minor in a subject as a prerequisite for or in conjunction with an education degree.[2]

Teaching credential reforms that incorporate subject-matter knowledge have also been enacted in federal education policy. Most recently, the Elementary and Secondary Education Act of 1965 (ESEA), as amended by the No Child Left Behind Act of 2001 (NCLB) (P.L. 107-110), requires that all public school teachers, in states participating in the ESEA Title I-A program for Education of the Disadvantaged, be *highly qualified* by demonstrating subject knowledge for their teaching level.

Elementary school teachers must show knowledge of basic elementary school curricular areas. Middle and secondary school teachers must demonstrate a high level of competency in all subject areas taught. Subject-matter knowledge and competency may be demonstrated by passing a state certification exam or licensing test in the relevant subject(s).[3]

One of the major goals of NCLB is to raise the achievement of students who currently fail to meet grade-level proficiency standards. Since student achievement has been shown to be dependent in large part on teacher quality, the law seeks to improve achievement by setting higher minimum teacher quality requirements. In complying with the law, schools are prevented from hiring substandard teachers, such as those with emergency or provisional certification, those without a baccalaureate degree, or those with limited subject knowledge.

For some time, it was thought that schools hired substandard teachers because a shortage existed in the overall supply of qualified teachers. That idea has been challenged in recent years by research that revealed the shortage is in fact a distribution problem. Some so-called "hard-to-staff" schools find it difficult to maintain a staff of qualified teachers, while other schools have an adequate supply (and in some cases an oversupply) of quality teachers.[4]

The reasons for the uneven distribution in the teacher supply are still a matter of debate. Some argue that rules providing priority in reassignment options to teachers with seniority and the late decision deadline given to resigning teachers relegates the least-qualified teachers to less desirable schools. Others point to working conditions and other factors that make these schools less desirable to quality teachers in the first place. Whatever the reasons for the uneven distribution of quality teachers, the persistence of hard-to-staff schools may undermine the impact of NCLB teacher quality standards in reducing the student achievement gap.

This report examines implementation of NCLB requirement of a highly qualified teacher in every public school classroom. The first section of the report describes the HQT requirement and how it has been specified through regulation, guidance, and policy statements issued by the Education Department (ED). In the second section, the report analyzes data from a national survey of schools to assess the extent to which they are meeting the NCLB challenge. Finally, the report discusses issues regarding these requirements that may be considered as the ESEA reauthorization process unfolds during the 110th Congress.

THE HIGHLY QUALIFIED TEACHER REQUIREMENT

NCLB requires that each state educational agency (SEA) receiving ESEA Title I, Part A funding (compensatory education of disadvantaged students) must have a plan to ensure that, by no later than the end of the 2005-2006 school year, all public school teachers teaching in core academic subjects within the state will meet the definition of a *highly qualified teacher* (HQT).

Definition of a Highly Qualified Teacher

According to ESEA, Section 9101(23), the definition of an HQT has two basic components. First, to be deemed highly qualified, a teacher must possess full state teaching certification (i.e., must not have had any certification requirements waived on an emergency, temporary, or provisional basis) as well as a baccalaureate degree. The second component of the definition is that an HQT must demonstrate subject-matter knowledge in the areas that she or he teaches. The manner in which teachers satisfy the second component depends on the extent of their teaching experience and the level at which they teach. These subject knowledge requirements are as follows:

- New elementary school teachers must pass a rigorous state test demonstrating subject knowledge and teaching skills in reading, writing, math, and other basic elementary school curricular areas.
- New middle or secondary school teachers must demonstrate a high level of competency in all subjects taught by (1) passing rigorous state academic tests in those subjects, or (2) completing an academic major (or equivalent course work), graduate degree, or advanced certification in each subject taught.
- Experienced school teachers must meet (1) the requirements described above for new teachers (depending upon his or her level of instruction), or (2) demonstrate competency in all subjects taught using a "high objective uniform state standard of evaluation" (HOUSSE).

These provisions indicate that the tests used to demonstrate subject-matter knowledge may include state certification or licensing exams. Section 9101(23) states that a demonstration of subject-matter knowledge by an elementary school teacher "may consist of passing a State-required certification or licensing test or tests in reading, writing, mathematics, and other areas of the basic elementary school curriculum." For a middle or secondary school teacher, Section 9101(23) states that a demonstration of subject-matter knowledge "may consist of a passing level of performance on a State-required certification or licensing test or tests in each of the academic subjects in which the teacher teaches."

Implementing the Definition

Since passage of NCLB, ED has further specified the HQT definition through regulation, non-regulatory guidance, and other means. In general, these policy statements address concerns about the scope and application of the HQT requirements. Among a wide variety of implementation issues, ED has sought to clarify what constitutes "core" subject matter, how states should develop and apply a HOUSSE, how the HQT requirements may be differentially applied to different types of teachers and in different types of educational settings, and when various aspects of the requirement must be completed.

Subject Matter

Early in the implementation of these provisions, some asked whether they apply to *all* teachers, including vocational education teachers, special education teachers, or others not teaching core academic subjects. According to ESEA Section 9101(11), "The term 'core academic subjects' means English, reading or language arts, mathematics, science, foreign languages, civics and government, economics, arts, history, and geography." Final regulations for the Title I program published on December 2, 2002, in the *Federal Register* apply these requirements only to core academic subject teachers. ED noted that these requirements would apply to a vocational education teacher or a special education teacher providing instruction in a core academic subject.[5]

ED addressed other subject matter issues in subsequent guidance and policy letters. A March 2004 policy announcement modified earlier non-regulatory guidance (issued in January 2004), which stated that science teachers teaching more than one field of science (e.g., biology and chemistry) would have to be highly qualified in each of the fields taught. Under the new flexibility, states determine whether science teachers need to be highly qualified in each science field they teach or highly qualified in science in general, based on how the state currently certifies teachers in these subject areas.

This new flexibility, along with other changes, was incorporated into the latest revised non-regulatory guidance issued on August 3, 2005.[6] The guidance clarifies that social studies is not considered a core subject and that certification in social studies or possession of a "composite social studies degree" does not necessarily indicate that a teacher is highly qualified to teach related subjects (e.g., economics and history). States are to determine whether a social science teacher is qualified to teach the specific subject he or she is assigned to teach.

High Objective Uniform State Standard of Evaluation (HOUSSE)

According to NCLB, a teacher who is not new to the teaching profession may demonstrate subject matter knowledge through the states' HOUSSE method. In defining its HOUSSE, the SEA must set standards for both grade appropriate academic subject knowledge and teaching skills that are aligned with challenging state academic and student achievement standards. The HOUSSE must provide objective information about teachers' content knowledge in all subjects taught and be applied uniformly statewide to all teachers in the same subjects and grade levels. Finally, the statute states that the HOUSSE may use multiple measures of teacher competency and may consider, but not be based primarily on, time teaching the relevant subjects.

Non-regulatory guidance, published on September 12, 2003, included suggestions on the development of HOUSSE procedures. According to the guidance, states should consider several factors when developing their HOUSSE procedures, including whether the proposed HOUSSE measures provide an "objective" way of determining whether a teacher has adequate subject-matter knowledge. The latest (August 2005) guidance defines "new" teachers as those with less than one year of teaching experience and teachers who are "not new" as those with more than one year of experience. However, the guidance indicates that states have the authority to determine who is new to the profession and who is not. States may also design their HOUSSE procedures to allow a teacher to go through the process a single time to demonstrate competency in multiple subjects.

Different Teachers

NCLB states that full certification includes "certification obtained through alternative routes to certification." The December 2002 final regulations indicated that teachers who were *participating* in an alternative certification program will be considered highly qualified on a provisional basis. Such teachers have a maximum of three years in which to become fully certified without being in violation of the highly qualified requirements regarding certification. This allowance is made only for a teacher in an alternative certification program who is receiving high-quality professional development, intensive supervision, and is making satisfactory progress toward full certification.

Concerns had been raised that the HQT requirements would limit participation in international teacher exchange programs. In a policy letter issued on March 24, 2003, the Secretary addressed these concerns by indicating how teachers from other countries could be considered highly qualified in the state in which they teach. The Secretary pointed out that each state has the full authority to define and enforce its own requirements for certification and licensure and make accommodations for foreign teachers. Accommodations could also be made in developing tests and other ways of demonstrating subject-matter expertise. In making this point, the Secretary clarified that one such demonstration provided in the law is coursework equivalent to an academic major.

These changes were included in the September 2003 updated guidance, along with clarification on the issue of middle school teachers. When determining whether teachers of core academic subjects in grades 6 through 8 should meet competency requirements for elementary or middle school teachers, the guidance advises states to "examine the degree of rigor and technicality of the subject matter that a teacher will need to know in relation to the state's content standards and academic achievement standards for the subjects in those grade levels." In addition, states may choose to consider teachers with middle school certification to be "highly qualified," and states may approve tests that are specifically developed for middle school teachers if the tests are "rigorous content-area assessments that are developed specifically for middle school teachers and aligned with middle school content and academic standards."

Different Settings

In a March 31, 2004 policy letter, the Secretary announced that additional flexibility could be applied in the implementation of the HQT requirements with regard to teachers in small rural school districts.[7] In small rural districts, ED provided that teachers teaching core academic subjects who meet the highly qualified requirements in at least one of the subject areas they teach may have an additional three years to meet these requirements in the other subjects they might teach. For *current* teachers, this three-year grace period began with the 2004-2005 school year, meaning that rather than facing a deadline of the end of the 2005-2006 school year to be highly qualified in all core subjects taught, current rural teachers may have until the end of the 2006-2007 school year. For *newly hired* teachers, a full three-year grace period can be provided from the date of hiring. But those newly hired teachers will have to be highly qualified in one of their core subject areas when hired. States decide whether to offer this flexibility to eligible rural districts.

Section 9101(23) states that charter school teachers must meet "the requirements set forth in the State's public charter school law." ED's guidance clarifies that this only refers to the requirements for certification and indicates that such teachers must meet all other HQT requirements. The guidance also states that teachers in juvenile and correctional institutions or "other alternative settings" must meet HQT standards only if such settings are considered LEAs under state law.

Deadlines for Implementation

Each SEA was to submit its plan to meet the HQT deadline along with its Consolidated State Application for State Grants on July 12, 2002.[8] The plan must establish annual measurable objectives for each local educational agency (LEA) and school that, at a minimum, include annual increases in the percentage of HQTs at each LEA and school to ensure that the 2005-2006 deadline is met. In turn, each LEA must also have a plan to meet this deadline. In addition, beginning with the first day of the 2002-2003 school year, any LEA receiving ESEA Title I funding must ensure that all teachers hired after that date who are teaching in Title I-supported programs are highly qualified. States and LEAs must also submit annual reports to ED describing progress on the state-set annual objectives.

The Consolidated State Performance Reports (CSPR), for the 2003-2004 school year due in January of 2005, were to contain the first data on the status of meeting the HQT requirement. However, ED reported widespread problems in state data systems and offered a series of regional data workshops to support states in collecting data.[9] This includes the additional data on teachers who are not highly qualified that was required to be submitted in the January 2006 CSPR. ED announced these workshops in a policy letter to chief state school officers dated October 21, 2005.

The letter also announced additional flexibility in meeting the HQT deadline. The Secretary stated that the letter's purpose was "to assure you that States that do not quite reach the 100% goal by the end of the 2005-06 school year will not lose federal funds if they are implementing the law and making a good-faith effort to reach the HQT goal in NCLB as soon as possible."[10] Instead, states that "meet the law's requirements and the Department's expectations in these areas but fall short of having highly qualified teachers in every classroom" would be given an additional year to reach the 100% goal.

Figure 1 provides a graphic diagram of the major HQT requirements as defined in NCLB and further specified in ED regulation and guidance.

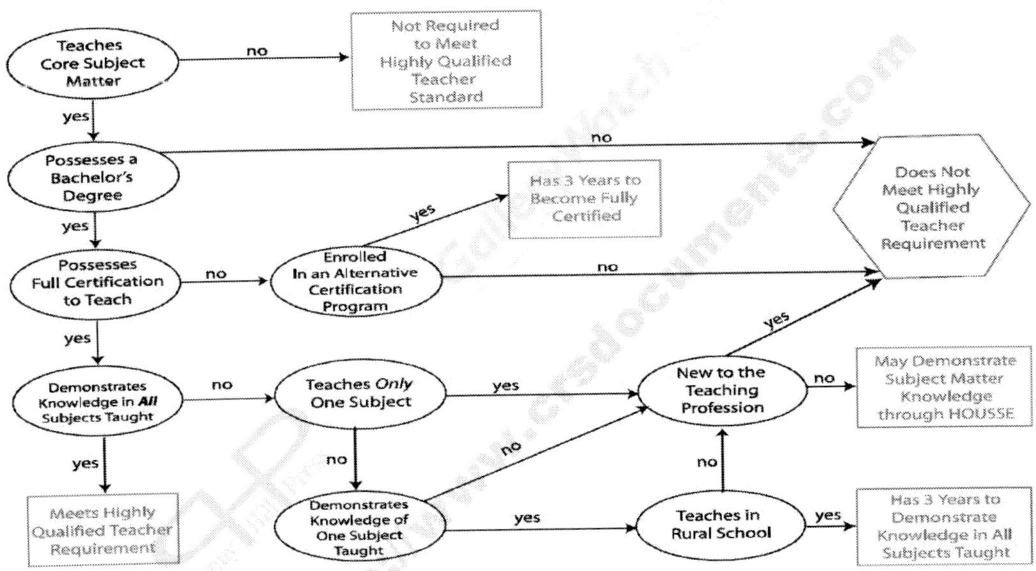

Figure 1. Diagram of Highly Qualified Teacher Requirement.

Meeting the Highly Qualified Teacher Challenge

Given the aforementioned problems with state HQT data systems, the only source of reliable information on teacher quality comes from survey data. The Schools and Staffing Survey (SASS) conducted by ED's National Center for Education Statistics collects data on teacher, school, and district characteristics from a very large, representative sample of schools throughout the country.[11] This analysis uses SASS data collected during the 1999-2000 school year.[12] The survey asked teachers who taught during that school year a series of questions about their teaching experience, assignments, education, and certification.

The SASS survey estimates that just under 3 million teachers were employed during the 1999-2000 school year.[13] That was the first year of teaching for roughly 173,000 (5.8%) of the 3 million teachers. Virtually all teachers (99.3%) held a baccalaureate degree at the time of the survey; the large majority (95.9%) also held some form of state teaching certification. Most teachers (91.4%) were employed full-time in 1999-2000; of the remainder, 3.0% worked part-time, 3.5% split time between more than one school, and 2.2% were "non-regular" teachers consisting mostly of administrators and librarians who also taught a class that year (the latter group are omitted from the analysis in this report).[14]

Some teachers teach more than one grade level, and school districts vary in how they combine grade levels; however, ED has developed a scheme to uniformly classify teachers across the country as either *elementary*, *middle*, or *secondary*.[15] In 1999-2000, 43% of teachers were classified as elementary, 26% as middle, 30% as secondary, and 1% as "other." Nearly one-third of all teachers (29.7%) did not teach a "core" academic subject during the 1999-2000 school year.[16] These non-core teachers are not subject to the HQT requirement and are omitted from this analysis.[17]

Core Subject Teachers

Of the 2.1 million teachers who taught at least one core subject in 1999-2000, 1.73 million (83.6%) taught a single subject and 339,000 (16.4%) taught two subjects.[18] Nine in ten single-subject teachers (91.4%) reported that they held full state certification in the subject they taught.[19] Half of all two-subject teachers (49.9%) reported that they held full state certification in both of their subjects. Taken together, 84.5% of all single and two-subject teachers held a baccalaureate degree and reported being certified in the subject(s) they teach. Since NCLB considers state certification in all fields taught adequate demonstration of subject-matter knowledge, these data suggest that prior to the passage of NCLB, more than eight out of ten teachers met the HQT requirement. Table 1 presents the qualifications of core subject teachers for the 1999-2000 school year.

Table 1. Qualifications of Core Subject Teachers, 1999-2000

	Number	Percent
Core Subject Teachers	2,068,306	100%
Certified in all Subjects Taught	1,747,343	84.5
In Alternative Certification Program	64,009	3.1
Certified in 1 of 2 Subjects and SRSA	9,246	0.4
Total of Highly Qualified Teachers	1,820,598	88.0
Certified in 1 of 2 Subjects and non-SRSA	117,536	5.7
Certified in Other Subject or Other State	19,093	0.9
Not Certified	75,924	3.7
Temporary or Emergency Certification	31,662	1.5
No Baccalaureate Degree	3,547	0.2
Total of Underqualified Teachers	247,708	12.0

Source: CRS analysis of the U.S. Department of Education, National Center for Education Statistics' 1999-2000 Schools and Staffing Survey.

An additional 3.1% of all teachers were participating in an alternative certification program at the time of the survey. Such teachers have three years to complete their program and become fully certified. Another 6.1% of all teachers taught two subjects but only held certification in one. About one in 10 of these teachers were located in LEAs eligible for participation in the Small Rural School Achievement (SRSA) program (ESEA Title VI-B).[20] According to the guidance discussed above, these teachers have additional time to demonstrate subject-matter knowledge in the field in which they are not highly qualified —

one year in the case of veteran teachers and three years for new teachers. Thus, a total of 3.5% of all 1999-2000 teachers would have been temporarily deemed highly qualified teachers (combining those in alternative certification programs and those in SRSA schools who were uncertified in one of their two subjects).

Underqualified Teachers

The data presented in the previous two paragraphs indicate that — with 84.5% HQTs and 3.5% temporarily HQTs — just over one in ten teachers (12.0%) were not highly qualified during the 1999-2000 school year. These *underqualified teachers* (UQTs) can be divided up as follows: (1) non-SRSA teachers who taught two subjects but only held certification in one (5.7% of all teachers), (2) teachers who were not certified in the subjects(s) they taught but held certification in another field or state (0.9% of all teachers), (3) those who held no certification at all (3.7% of all teachers), (4) teachers who held temporary or emergency certification (1.5% of all teachers), and (5) those who did not have a baccalaureate degree (0.2% of all teachers).

As identified by the SASS survey, UQTs differ from HQTs in many respects. Demographic characteristics for each group are compared in table 2. HQTs were more likely to teach elementary school than middle or secondary school. Of all elementary school teachers, 94.0% were highly qualified (HQ), compared to 76.8% of middle school teachers and 85.3% of secondary school teachers. Female teachers were slightly more likely to be HQ than male teachers (89.0%, compared to 84.4%). White teachers were more likely to be HQ than non-white teachers. Among white teachers, 89.4% were HQ, compared to 84.2% of Asian teachers, 80.4% of black teachers, and 78.4% of Hispanic teachers. Of all the core subjects, science teachers were the least likely to be HQ (77.3%), followed by English teachers (81.8%) and math teachers (82.6%). Teachers with less than five years of teaching experience at the time of the survey were less likely to be HQ than those with five or more years of experience (77.9%, compared to 90.7%).

Table 2. Demographic Characteristics by Teacher Qualifications

Characteristic	Highly Qualified Teachers	Underqualified Teachers
All Core Subject Teachers	88.0%	12.0%
Teaching Level		
Elementary	94.0	6.0
Middle	76.8	23.2
Secondary	85.3	14.7
Sex		
Female	89.0	11.0
Male	84.4	15.6
Race/Ethnicity		
White,Nnon-Hispanic	89.4	10.6
Black, Non-Hispanic	80.4	19.6
Asian, Non-Hispanic	84.2	15.8
Hispanic	78.4	21.6

Table 2. (Continued)

Characteristic	Highly Qualified Teachers	Underqualified Teachers
Main Assignment		
Kindergarten-Elem.	95.1	4.9
Art	90.4	9.6
Math	82.6	17.4
Social studies	84.6	15.4
English	81.8	18.2
Foreign languages	85.6	14.4
Science	77.3	22.7
Other	49.4	50.6
Teaching Experience		
less than Five Years	77.9	22.1
Five Years or More	90.7	9.3

Source: CRS analysis of the U.S. Department of Education, National Center for Education Statistics' 1999-2000 Schools and Staffing Survey.

Table 3. School Characteristics by Teacher Qualifications

Characteristic	Highly Qualified Teachers	Underqualified Teachers
All Core Subject Teachers	88.0%	12.0%
SRSA Schools	95.3	4.7
Urbanicity		
Central City	86.4	13.6
Urban Fringe	88.5	11.5
Small Town	88.9	11.1
Size		
Less than 100 Students	86.1	13.9
100-999 Students	89.2	10.8
1,000 or More Students	84.3	15.7
Minority enrollment		
Less than 20%	91.0	9.0
20% or More	85.5	14.5
LEP enrollment		
Less than 20%	88.6	11.4
20% or More	82.6	17.4
Minority teachers		
Less than 20%	89.4	10.6
20% or More	83.0	17.0

Source: CRS analysis of the U.S. Department of Education, National Center for Education Statistics' 1999-2000 Schools and Staffing Survey.

The characteristics of schools at which HQTs and UQTs taught during the 1999-2000 school year also differ. School characteristics for each group are presented in table 3. HQTs were less likely to teach at schools in the SRSA program and more likely to teach in urban schools. Among schools in the SRSA program, 95.3% were HQT, compared to 87.7% in non-SRSA schools. However, using ED's "urbanicity" designation of schools, "small town" schools, and "urban fringe" schools were equally likely to employ HQTs (88.9% and 88.5%, respectively), whereas schools in the "central city" category were less likely to employ HQTs (86.4%). HQTs were more likely to teach at medium-sized schools than at large or small schools. Among schools with enrollment below 100 students or above 999 students, 86.1% and 84.3%, respectively, were HQT; compared to 89.2% at schools with enrollment between

100 and 999. HQTs were more likely to teach at schools with low minority and limited English proficient (LEP) enrollment. Schools with less than 20% minority enrollment employed 91.0% HQT, compared to 85.5% at those with 20% or greater minority enrollment. Schools with less than 20% LEP enrollment employed 88.6% HQT, compared to 82.6% at those with 20% or greater LEP enrollment. Finally, HQTs were more likely to teach at schools with fewer minority teachers. Schools with less than 20% minority teachers employed 89.4% HQT, compared to 83.0% at schools with 20% or greater minority teachers.

Summary of Findings

This analysis indicates that a large majority of core subject-matter teachers would have met the HQT definition prior to enactment of NCLB. That is, they possessed a baccalaureate degree, regular certification, and subject-matter knowledge — demonstrating subject-matter knowledge by being certified to teach all subjects taught during the 1999-2000 school year. Those who did not meet the HQT standard fell into two main groups: (1) those who taught two subjects and only held certification in one, or (2) those who were insufficiently or improperly certified (i.e., they had no certification, held a temporary or emergency certification, or they were certified in a subject or state in which they do not teach).

This analysis reveals that UQTs were more likely to be male, non-white, and have fewer than five years of teaching experience. UQTs were less likely to report "Kindergarten/Elementary" and "Art" as their main teaching assignment. The subject areas most often reported by UQTs as their main assignment were "science," "English," and "math." UQTs were more likely to be classified by ED as middle school teachers. UQTs are less likely teach in schools designated as eligible for the SRSA program. Instead, UQTs are more likely to teach in a "central city" location at either a very small or very large school. UQTs also are more likely to teach in schools with high minority and LEP enrollments, as well as in schools with a large proportion of minority teachers.

As stated above, half of UQTs (5.7% of all teachers) taught two subjects but were only certified in one. Another small portion of UQTs (0.9% of all teachers) held certification in a subject or state in which they were not teaching. Nine in 10 of these teachers were "veteran" teachers (i.e., had more that one year of teaching experience at the time of the survey) and, therefore, could obtain HQT status through the HOUSSE method.

State HOUSSE Plans

All 50 states have submitted their HOUSSE plans for evaluating experienced teachers who do not meet the HQT requirements laid out above. ED has responded to these plans and provided feedback in areas where it feels they do not meet the HQT standard. ED has also conducted monitoring and site visits to most SEAs and several LEAs to collect information and provide advice on HOUSSE implementation. ED has not made HOUSSE plans available to the public; however, a few organizations are tracking each state's development of these systems.[21] A review of the available information reveals that state HOUSSE plans employ a few common strategies for evaluating veteran teachers. Most plans involve the use of a points system for rating teachers on a scale of teacher quality. Many states assess their teachers using existing performance evaluation systems. The professional activities common across all HOUSSE plans include coursework, teaching experience, and professional development.

Points System

The National Council on Teacher Quality (NCTQ) reported that 30 state HOUSSE plans include a point system (see the December 2004 report cited in footnote 21). In this method, teachers accumulate points for engaging in activities thought to improve teaching and subject-matter knowledge. Teachers are required to submit documentation of these activities, which is reviewed by a trained evaluator or administrator. Various activities are worth different point amounts and, generally, 100 points are required to be considered highly qualified (points can usually be earned retroactively). Some states require that teachers first accrue points for academic work in order to become eligible to accrue points for other activities. Most activities have a cap on the maximum number of points that can be awarded in a particular category. Some states have a short list of three or four activities, while other states have a long list of eligible activities in a few general categories.

Performance Evaluation

The NCTQ report indicates that seven states use annual teacher performance evaluations in their HOUSSE plan, although some have modified traditional criteria to fit NCLB requirements. Teachers are observed and evaluated based on a series of teaching criteria that include content knowledge. Some states have included measures of student achievement as part of the evaluation. Some states have one evaluation period per year conducted by a school administrator; others have regular peer evaluations in addition to an administrator's evaluation. Some states allow for consideration of past performance evaluations. Those receiving an acceptable level of performance are considered to meet the highly qualified requirement.

Professional Activities

Most state HOUSSE plans include three major categories of activities that count toward achieving HQT status: coursework, teaching experience, and professional development. In many states, college-level coursework in the area in which the teacher is assigned can be counted toward meeting all or part of the requirement. In states using a point system, points are often awarded in relation to the number of credit hours fulfilled. Possession of a baccalaureate major and the attainment of an advanced degree in the subject taught usually carries additional weight. Most states also give teachers credit toward meeting the HQT standard for their years of teaching experience. Some states require that performance evaluations accompany documentation of this experience and only give credit for years taught with positive evaluations. Points may be awarded for years, or groups of years, and are usually capped. Finally, states usually count professional development activities toward meeting their HOUSSE requirement.

These activities may include participation in workshops on teaching content, work toward National Board Certification, and involvement in school/teacher leadership.

Reauthorization Issues

The current funding authority for the ESEA will expire after FY2007.[22] Legislative action to reauthorize and amend the ESEA, along with the HQT requirements, will likely occur during the 110th Congress. Numerous proposals have already been forwarded that cover a number of important issues likely to be raised during the reauthorization process. Most of these proposals would amend the HQT definition or make exceptions for certain teachers or schools. Many of the proposals make changes similar to the waivers and increased flexibility already announced by ED.

Multiple Subject Teachers

Although the analysis in this report indicates that less than one in five teachers teaches more than one subject, those who did teach more than one subject were much less likely to be HQT. Among multiple subject teachers in this analysis, half did not meet the HQT standard. This small group — fewer than six percent of all teachers — may present a large problem for schools and states attempting to meet the 100% HQT requirement. Solutions have been proposed for certain kinds of schools (such as rural and hard-to-staff schools, discussed below); however, some proposals seek to address the problem for teachers in all schools generally. These amendments would allow teachers teaching multiple subjects to demonstrate knowledge in one subject area using the existing methods and provide a second method for other subject(s) taught. For example, multiple subject teachers who are HQT in one of their subjects could be given a certain amount of time to accumulate coursework equivalent to an academic minor in the subject(s) for which they lack sufficient knowledge.

Definition of Subject Matter

The issue of multiple subject teachers is in part created by the definition of subject matter in NCLB. Specifically, section 9101(11) of the statute states that, "The term 'core academic subjects' means, English, reading and language arts, mathematics, science, foreign languages, civics and government, economics, arts, history, and geography." As mentioned earlier, ED addressed issues related to science and social studies teachers in its non-regulatory guidance. States were given the authority to determine whether teachers qualified to teach in one field of science or social studies were qualified in other fields in those areas. Some have proposed legislative solutions that would recognize "generalist" certificates in these and other areas as proof of subject-matter knowledge.

Middle School Teachers

Many of the teachers found not to meet the HQT standard in this analysis were teaching middle school students. The problem posed by this group of teachers is that some have duties similar to elementary teachers, while others are more like secondary school teachers. That is, some middle school teachers work in so-called "self-contained" classroom settings where they are responsible for teaching multiple subjects to the same group of students. Meanwhile, other middle school teachers work in "departmental" settings, in which they teach the same subject to different groups of students over the course of a single day. According to NCLB, middle school teachers are to be treated like secondary school teachers with regard to demonstration of subject-matter expertise. Thus, those teaching multiple subjects in self-contained classrooms must be certified to teach in several subjects — or prove subject knowledge in each area by the other permitted means. The proposals to recognize "generalist" certification mentioned above would remedy this problem. Other proposals include expanding the allowable types of experience and forms of evaluation permitted in state HOUSSE methods for veteran middle school teachers.

Rural, Urban, and Poor Schools

This analysis revealed that UQTs are less likely to work in SRSA schools. SRSA schools are largely defined as those located in areas classified as "rural" according to the U.S. Census Bureau locale codes. However, other evidence suggests that rural schools are among the so-called "hard-to-staff" schools, which will have an especially difficult time meeting the 100% HQT requirement.[23] Part of the explanation for the disparity between these two conclusions rests in the definition of rurality. Specifically, ED analysis has found the Census locale code classifications of rural areas to be at best crude and in some cases grossly inaccurate.[24] One proposal would give rural schools until the 2009-2010 school year to meet the HQT deadline; however, the proposal would provide this option only to SRSA schools. Another proposal would give the Secretary the authority to waive the HQT requirement for any rural school that could demonstrate that the requirement would impose an undue hardship on the school because of population and geographic constraints.

This analysis revealed that "central city" schools have the highest rates of UQTs. Additional analysis has shown that schools in poor neighborhoods also have higher rates of UQTs.[25] Although no legislative amendments have been proposed to address issues regarding urban or poor schools, some of the proposals presented here that concern "hard-to-staff" schools could be adopted to relieve the burden imposed by the HQT requirement. However, given the high turnover rates at these schools, short-term waivers and deadline extensions may not provide sufficient relief. At the same time, such flexibility might weaken NCLB's emphasis on improving instructional quality — especially for disadvantaged pupils attending schools in high poverty areas.

References

[1] Michael B. Allen, *Eight Questions on Teacher Preparation: What Does the Research Say?*, Education Commission of the States, July 2003; Linda Darling-Hammond and Gary Sykes, "Wanted: A National Teacher Supply Policy for Education," *Education Policy Analysis Archives*, vol. 11, no. 33 (September 2003); Dan Goldhaber and Emily Anthony, "Can Teacher Quality Be Effectively Assessed?," The Urban Institute,

Research Paper no. 410958, April 27, 2004; Leslie G. Vandervoort and David C. Berliner, "National Board Certified Teachers and Their Students' Achievement," *Education Policy Analysis Archives*, vol. 12, no. 46, (September 2004); Eric A. Hanushek, et al., "The Market for Teacher Quality," National Bureau of Economic Research, Working Paper no. 11154, February 2005.

[2] The College of Education at the University of Kentucky provides a compilation of teacher certification requirements for all 50 states. The compilation is available online at [http://www.uky.edu/Education/TEP/usacert.html]. The National Association of State Directors of Teacher Education and Certification annually publishes a similar compilation, The NASDTEC Manual on the Preparation and Certification of Educational Personnel, that is available at [http://www.nasdtec.org].

[3] Teachers may also demonstrate knowledge by having majored in the relevant subject(s), and experienced teachers may do so through the HOUSSE method explained later in this report.

[4] Richard M. Ingersol, *Teacher Turnover, Teacher Shortages, and the Organization of Schools*, Center for the Study of Teaching and Policy, Research Report, January 2001; Patrick J. Murphy and Michael M. DeArmond, *From the Headlines to the Frontlines: The Teacher Shortage and Its Implications for Recruitment Policy*, Center on Reinventing Public Education, Research Paper, July 2003; the American Association for Employment in Education, *Educator Supply and Demand in the United States 2001*, Research Report, 2002; Recruiting New Teachers, Inc., *The Urban Teacher Challenge*, Research Report, January 2000.

[5] The application of HQT requirements to special education teachers was subsequently modified under the Individuals with Disabilities Education Act. For more information, see CRS Report RL32913, *The Individuals with Disabilities Education Act (IDEA): Interactions with Selected Provisions of the No Child Left Behind Act*, by Richard N. Apling and Nancy Lee Jones.

[6] The most recently revised ESEA Title II non-regulatory guidance is available online at [http://www.ed.gov/programs/teacherqual/guidance.doc].

[7] Rural school teachers are defined as those teaching in schools eligible for the Small Rural School Achievement (SRSA) Program (ESEA Title VI-B). The policy letter announcing this flexibility is available at [http://www.ed.gov/policy/elsec/guid/secletter/040331.html].

[8] Although some states have made their plans available to the public, the Secretary has yet to release the plans of any state.

[9] A GAO report dated July 2003 anticipated these data systems problems: U.S. Government Accountability Office, *No Child Left Behind Act: More Information Would Help States Determine Which Teachers Are Highly Qualified*, GAO-03-631.

[10] The Secretary's letter is available at [http://www.ed.gov/policy/elsec/guid/secletter/051021.html].

[11] The sample is drawn from ED's Common Core of Data, which contains virtually every school in the country.

[12] Data from the 2003-2004 survey are currently being analyzed and will be incorporated in a forthcoming update of this report.

[13] This figure does not include those employed as teacher aides (or *paraprofessionals*). Although NCLB does contain a separate series of requirements for paraprofessional quality, individuals employed to assist teachers were not included in the SASS sample.

[14] Since the use of long-term substitutes has received some attention, it is worth noting that 0.43% (or 12,826) of all 3 million teachers were employed as long-term substitutes. ED guidance recommends that substitutes meet HQT requirements; however, states need only notify parents if their child has been taught by a non-HQT substitute for more than four consecutive months.

[15] Teachers were assigned by SASS programmers in a manner consistent with the assignment of schools to elementary, middle, and secondary levels developed by the NCES in U.S. Department of Education, National Center for Education Statistics, *In the Middle: Characteristics of Public Schools with a Focus on Middle Schools*, NCES 2000-312, by Martha Naomi Alt and Susan P. Choy, MPR Associates, Inc., and Charles H. Hammer, Project Officer, Washington, D.C. July 2000 [http://nces.ed.gov/pubs2000/2000312.pdf].

[16] The areas defined as "core subjects" in this analysis are "Kindergarten/Elementary," "Art," "Mathematics," "Social studies," "English or language arts," "Foreign languages," and "Science." Although social studies is not contained in the statutory language, it is used in this analysis because it encompasses subjects that are in the statute; namely, economics, history, and geography.

[17] Special education teachers who teach a core subject are required to be HQT; however, most were omitted from this analysis due to the SASS instrument design. One in ten (11.4%) of all teachers reported "special education" as one of their subjects taught, but only 1.1% of all teachers reported teaching "special education" in addition to a core subject. Thus, only the latter group was included in this analysis.

[18] Additional analysis of SASS data reveal that only a small fraction (less that 2%) of these teachers taught more than two subjects in 1999-2000. Therefore, the analysis in this report only considers teachers' first two teaching assignments.

[19] It is important to note that the SASS data are self-reported. The responding teachers were simply asked whether they were certified in the subject(s) they taught. At the time of the survey, a handful of states did not include subject-matter testing as part of their certification exams and several other states only recently instituted subject-matter testing. Thus, it is difficult to determine how many of these teachers have demonstrated subject-matter knowledge through testing. The proportion meeting the HQT requirement may be lower than the SASS data predict; however, a review of preliminary HQT data made available on states' report cards suggest that the SASS over-estimation will not be substantial. This assessment was also corroborated by anecdotal evidence from ED monitoring visits, according to a February 27, 2006 phone conversation with an ED official.

[20] As mentioned earlier, multiple-subject teachers in SRSA schools who are HQT in one subject have up to three years to become highly qualified in the other subjects they teach.

[21] Three such organizations are the National Council on Teacher Quality (NCTQ), the Southern Regional Education Board (SREB), and the Education Commission of the States (ECS). These organizations have released the following reports on state HOUSSE plans —Kate Walsh and Emma Snyder, *Searching the Attic: How States Are*

Responding to the Nation's Goal of Placing a Highly Qualified Teacher in Every Classroom, NCTQ, Washington, D.C., Winter 2004; Lynn Cornett and Alice Anne Bailey, *Focus on "Highly Qualified" Teachers: SREB States Take Action*, SREB, Atlanta, Georgia, October 2003; Jennifer Azordegan, *Initial Findings and Major Questions About HOUSSE*, ECS, Denver, Colorado, January 2004. ECS also maintains websites that compile the latest HOUSSE information for each state.

[22] A one-year automatic extension of authorizations of appropriations is provided under the General Education Provisions Act.

[23] Based on anecdotal evidence from ED monitoring visits provided during a February 27, 2006 phone conversation with an ED official.

[24] Douglas E. Geverdt, *Review of NCES School Locale Tabulation and Analysis*, U.S. Census Bureau, Technical Memorandum, December 22, 2005.

[25] Wuejin Lu, Teacher Quality: A National Survey of Secondary Public School Teachers Using SASS 1999-2000, unpublished manuscript.

In: No Child Left Behind: Issues and Developments
Editor: P. H. Berkhart, pp. 121-130
ISBN: 978-1-60456-210-1

Chapter 6

EDUCATION OF LIMITED ENGLISH PROFICIENT AND RECENT IMMIGRANT STUDENTS: PROVISIONS IN THE NO CHILD LEFT BEHIND ACT OF 2001*

Jeffrey J. Kuenzi

ABSTRACT

The No Child Left Behind Act of 2001 (NCLBA, P.L. 107-110) represents a major overhaul of federal programs for the education of limited English proficient and recent immigrant students. Programs for bilingual and immigrant education under the Elementary and Secondary Education Act of 1965 (ESEA) were consolidated and underwent several important changes with regard to the funding mechanism, method of instructional delivery, and focus on educational outcomes and accountability.

The NCLBA consolidated several competitively awarded grants in the Bilingual Education Act and a formula grant in the Emergency Immigrant Education Act (ESEA, Title VII, Parts A and C) into a single population-based formula grant. The new Language Acquisition State Formula Grant Program (ESEA, Title III) allocates 80% of funding according to the population of limited English proficient (LEP) students and 20% according to the population of recently arriving immigrants.

The law gives state and local educational agencies greater flexibility in the design and administration of language instructional programs and removes language in Title VII that encouraged bilingual instruction methods (i.e., curricula that develop proficiency in more than one language). At the same time, the law develops and focuses greater attention to the achievement of English proficiency.

Among many amendments to pupil assessment, the NCLBA builds upon language in the 1994 ESEA amendments. The law increases the reporting requirements for language and academic assessments as well as the accommodations under which those assessments are given to LEP pupils. Recipients of Title III money are also subjected to greater accountability standards tied to Title I adequate yearly progress (AYP) provisions.

In the first year of its existence, funding for Title III was dramatically increased over the previous year's Title VII appropriation — from $460 million in FY2001 to $665

* Excerpted from CRS Report RL31315, dated January 11, 2007.

million in FY2002. Since that time, the appropriations for the program have remained stable — $684 million in FY2003, $681 million in FY2004, $676 million in FY2005, and $669 million in FY2006.

Title III, along with the rest of the ESEA, will likely be considered for reauthorization by the 110th Congress.

Introduction

The Language Acquisition State Grant Program under Title III of the Elementary and Secondary Education Act of 1965 (ESEA) as amended by the No Child Left Behind Act (NCLBA) contains provisions intended to address the specific educational needs of limited English proficient (LEP) students and students who have recently immigrated to the United States.[1] Title III represents a major overhaul of federal programs for LEP students formerly provided under ESEA, Title VII, Parts A and C.

One of the most significant policy changes made in this part of the law (P.L. 107-110) was the shift from several competitively awarded grants to a single population-based formula grant. State educational agencies (SEAs) and local educational agencies (LEAs) were also given greater flexibility in the design and administration of language instructional programs. At the same time, program objectives were more narrowly defined and were subject to new accountability standards as well as parental notification requirements. Appropriations for this program increased nearly 45% from $460 million in FY2001 to $665 million in FY2002 and leveled off at $686 million for FY2003, $681 million in FY2004, $676 million in FY2005, and $669 million in FY2006.

These amendments occurred at the end of a decade that saw two important and potentially conflicting developments with regard to the education of LEP students. The first concerns rapid growth of the non-native English speaking student population. The second involves increasing pressure to conduct assessments and hold schools accountable for academic achievement.

Demographic Trends

The population of foreign-born individuals residing in the United States increased by more than 50% during the 1990s — from 20 million in 1990 to 31 million in 2000.[2] In fact, the growth of this group accounts for nearly half of the nation's overall population growth during the decade — from 249 to 274 million.

This population trend has been nearly matched by a 43% increase in the number of U.S. residents who report having poor English-speaking ability. Of the 45 million individuals who spoke a language other than English at home in 2000, 20 million (44%) said they spoke English less than "very well." In 1990, of the 32 million who spoke non-English languages at home, 14 million (44%) spoke English less than "very well."[3]

School enrollment data suggest that the increase in LEP students has been even more rapid. The U.S. Department of Education's National Clearinghouse for Bilingual Education estimates that LEP enrollment in U.S. schools during the 1999-2000 academic year was 4 million students — up from 2 million during the 1989-1990 academic year.[4]

Student Assessment

Simultaneous with the influx of immigrants and students with limited English skills, there has been growing pressure on SEAs and LEAs to develop academic assessments and require that schools meet performance standards. In addition to education policies adopted in most states,[5] the Improving America's Schools Act of 1994 (IASA, P.L. 103-382) directed states to develop and implement "standards-based" assessments. In the late 1990s, schools were facing increasing pressure to test their students and, in some cases, demonstrate improvement in student achievement.

The IASA also required "reasonable adaptations and accommodations" be made for LEP pupils. The purpose of these accommodations was to provide an accurate and reliable measure of students' knowledge in core academic areas (in subjects other than English, such as math and science). The NCLBA also contains such accommodations but stipulates that they can only be made during an LEP pupil's first three years in U.S. schools. After three consecutive years in U.S. schools, LEP students are to be assessed in English.[6]

TITLE III PROVISIONS

The NCLBA also raised the stakes for poor student assessment outcomes and failure to meet progressively higher levels of academic performance. Schools must develop academic standards, establish levels of adequate yearly progress (AYP), and face serious consequences for failing to achieve that progress.[7] LEP students and the LEAs that serve them face particularly difficult challenges in achieving the goals set by the NCLBA.

According to the conference report (H.Rept. 107-334) for the legislation, the specific goals set by Title III are to:

- help ensure that LEP and recent immigrant children develop English proficiency,
- assist these students in achieving academic standards in core subject matter,
- develop language instruction education programs that assist SEAs and LEAs in teaching LEP and recent immigrant students,
- assist in preparing students to enter all-English instruction settings,
- promote parental and community participation in these programs,
- streamline programs designed to provide language instruction,
- hold SEAs and LEAs accountable for annual increases in English proficiency and core academic content, and
- provide SEAs and LEAs flexibility in implementing these programs.

Formula Grants

To meet these goals, the NCBLA created an entirely new way of funding programs that serve LEP students. That is, Title III consolidated several Title VII programs into a single formula grant program (for fiscal years in which appropriations reach or exceed $650 million).[8]

Grants to States

Grants are distributed to the 50 states, the District of Columbia, and Puerto Rico based on proportions of their LEP and recent immigrant populations relative to national counts of these populations. No state can receive a grant less than $500,000.[9] The grant to Puerto Rico cannot exceed 0.5% of the total available for state distribution. Each state's share of the funds available for distribution (i.e., after continuation awards and reservations are removed) is described by the following equation:

$$State\_Share = \left(\frac{State\_LEP\_Pop.}{U.S.\_LEP\_Pop.}\right) * 0.8 + \left(\frac{State\_RIM\_Pop.}{U.S.\_RIM\_Pop.}\right) * 0.2$$

where:

"State_LEP_Pop." equals the number of LEP children in a state, "State_RIM_Pop." equals the number of recent immigrant children in a state, "U.S._LEP_Pop." equals the number of LEP children in all states, and "U.S._RIM_Pop." equals the number of recent immigrant children in all states.

Continuation Awards and Reservations

LEAs and other eligible recipients of Title VII grants under Subparts 1 and 3 of Parts A and C whose grants have not yet expired will continue to receive funds. These continuations as well as three reservations are set aside before state grants are distributed. The first reservation, a set-aside of 6.5%, provides (1) support for professional development through the National Professional Development Project and (2) continued funding of the National Clearinghouse for Bilingual Education (renamed National Clearinghouse for English Language Acquisition and Language Instruction Programs). A second set-aside of 0.5% (or $5,000,000, whichever is greater) provides grants to schools that predominantly serve Native American and Alaska Native children. A third set-aside of 0.5% is reserved for schools in the Outlying Areas.

Data for Determinations

The Secretary is given the discretion to determine (between U.S. Census Bureau data and state-submitted data) the most timely and accurate source of data on which to base grant distribution. In the implementation thus far, population estimates for the number of LEP children were taken both from data available through the Census Bureau while estimates for the number of recent immigrant children were taken from data submitted by SEAs.

Subgrants to Eligible Entities

Within-state distribution of funds is based on the number of LEP children only — regardless of their immigrant status. However, states can reserve up to 15% for grants to eligible entities containing schools that have recently experienced large influxes of immigrant children. An eligible entity is defined as one or more LEAs in collaboration with an institution of higher education, a community-based organization, or an SEA. Before formula allocation, SEAs can reserve an additional 5% for state activities such as professional development, planning, evaluation, administration, technical assistance, and the like. The minimum grant to an eligible entity (hereafter referred to simply as an LEA) is $10,000.

Flexibility and Accountability

Title III also gave LEAs the autonomy to create local educational plans and established accountability provisions to be enforced by the Secretary of the U.S. Education Department (ED).

Local Plans

Local control of these plans is intended to give LEAs the flexibility to cater programs to the strengths and needs of their teachers and students. To receive a grant, each LEA must submit a plan to its SEA describing how it intends to use the funds for language instruction programs and activities designed to meet the goals and objectives laid out in Titles I and III. No specific methods of instruction are mandated under Title III. For example, schools are not required to teach students in their native language.[10]

Reporting Requirements

On the contrary, according to Section 3121(c)(1)(B), LEAs receiving Title III funds must submit program evaluations that report on LEP students who "have transitioned into classrooms not tailored to limited English proficient children." These evaluations, submitted at the end of every second fiscal year, must report data on the number of LEP students participating in language acquisition programs and the proportion of these students who have transitioned out of these programs. After approving these LEA plans and reports, SEAs must submit them to the ED for approval.

Academic and LEP Assessments

Title I of the ESEA requires that LEAs, "will, beginning not later than school year 2002-2003, provide for an annual assessment of English proficiency (measuring students' oral language, reading, and writing skills in English) of all students with limited English proficiency" (§1111(b)(7)). In addition to these assessments that test for limited English proficiency, academic assessments of students' skills in math as well as reading and language arts are required of all students. LEP student may receive language accommodations for the math portion of the assessment; however, those who have attended U.S. schools for three consecutive years must take reading and language arts assessments using tests written in English.[11]

Achievement Objectives

SEAs must develop annual measurable achievement objectives that reflect (1) the amount of time individual children are enrolled in programs, (2) annual increases in the number or percentage of children learning English, and (3) the number or percentage of students receiving waivers for reading or language arts assessments. These objectives are all tied to provisions for assessments and adequate yearly progress under Title I, Part A, Section 1111(b).[12] Three exceptions to these objectives can be made for LEAs that (1) experience significant increases in the number of LEP and immigrant children, (2) enroll a "statistically significant" number of immigrants who lacked access to education in their home country, or (3) enroll a "statistically significant" number of immigrants seeking refuge from war or natural disaster (§3122(a)(3)(B)).

Accountability Provisions

SEAs that find LEAs failing to meet these objectives for two consecutive years can require the LEA to develop an improvement plan. The SEA must provide technical assistance and consult with the failing LEA during the development and implementation of this plan. LEAs found to be failing for four consecutive years can be forced to modify their language instruction program, have their funds withdrawn, and have relevant personnel replaced by the SEA.[13]

Parental Notification

In addition to requiring LEAs to develop their local plans in consultation with parents and community groups, Title III provisions require that LEAs inform parents within 30 days of the beginning of the school year (or two weeks during the school year) if their child is identified for participation in a language instruction program. LEAs must also describe to such parents several aspects of the program, including the reasons for their child's LEP classification, their child's level of English proficiency, the methods of instruction and exit requirements of the program, and their right to remove their child from the program.[14]

ED Policy Implementation

In February of 2003, ED issued non-regulatory guidance on the Title III state grant program.[15] This was the second piece of non-regulatory guidance — the first explained what SEAs and LEAs had to include in their grant applications. The second document laid out the standards, assessments, and accountability provisions described in the pages above.

ED has more recently announced two "new policies" regarding the implementation of the academic assessment and AYP provisions of the NCLBA.[16] In a February 19, 2004 press conference, the Secretary described these new policies as follows:

> The new flexibility will allow LEP students, during their first year of enrollment in U.S. schools, to have the option of taking the reading/language arts content assessment in addition to taking the English language proficiency assessment. They would take the mathematics assessment, with accommodations as appropriate. States may, but would not be required to, include results from the mathematics and, if given, reading/language arts content assessments in AYP calculations.
>
> Since LEP students exit the LEP subgroup once they attain English language proficiency, states may have difficulty demonstrating improvements on state assessments for these students. Accordingly, the other new flexibility would, for AYP calculations, allow states for up to two years to include in the LEP subgroup students who have attained English proficiency.[17]

By exercising the option not to give first-year LEP students the reading/language arts assessment, LEAs could more easily meet the requirement in the AYP provisions that at least

95% of all pupils in each demographic group within each school must be included in assessments.[18] Waiving the requirement that these first-year LEP pupil content assessments be counted in AYP calculations might also make meeting the requirements easier. In the later stages of AYP implementation (as states try to meet progressively higher levels of performance), doing so would presumably increase the proportion of LEP students scoring at an adequately high level.[19]

Exercising the second policy option would seem to have a definite positive effect on state's ability to meet AYP requirements. Former LEP students recently moved out of that subgroup would presumably score lower on average (particularly on reading assessments) than those who never were classified as LEP. Thus, including former LEP pupil assessments with those a non-LEP subgroup would lower that subgroup's average score. Likewise, including former LEP pupil assessments with those still in the LEP subgroup would raise that subgroup's average score.

The first of these new policies might have the effect of buffering states and LEAs, in particular, from the effects caused by a large influx of LEP in-migrants from other areas. Being able to hold the new students out of AYP calculations would allow such LEAs to demonstrate the progress they've made with the LEP students that have been in their schools for a year or two. The second of these new policies will have the effect of smoothing the requirement that schools must transition LEP pupils into non-LEP classrooms. That is, it may remove one disincentive to reclassifying LEP students as non-LEP students.

FUNDING

Table 1 shows the formula-based allocation of these funds to each state for the last three fiscal years. Note that these estimates were produced on October 25, 2006, and thus were based on the President's FY2006 request of $675,765,000 rather than the actual FY2006 appropriation of $669,007,350.

Table 1. Language Acquisition State Grants

State or other area	2004 Actual	2005 Estimate	2006 Estimate	Change from 2005 estimate
Alabama	$1,878,554	$2,969,385	$3,337,650	$368,265
Alaska	$86,161	$835,169	$506,735	-$328,434
Arizona	$16,453,934	$16,053,667	$18,628,864	$2,575,197
Arkansas	$1,871,562	$1,986,077	$2,170,133	$184,056
California	$161,549,115	$149,565,827	$167,446,440	$17,880,613
Colorado	$7,069,901	$9,947,707	$11,277,872	$1,330,165
Connecticut	$5,380,812	$4,440,248	$4,784,676	$344,428
Delaware	$725,465	$876,486	$889,114	$12,628
District of Columbia	$680,354	$922,000	$947,074	$25,074
Florida	$36,272,809	$38,999,401	$39,451,135	$451,734
Georgia	$11,254,952	$13,281,802	$10,873,006	-$2,408,796
Hawaii	$2,186,577	$1,645,216	$2,254,592	$609,376
Idaho	$1,297,826	$2,107,363	$1,401,894	-$705,469
Illinois	$25,929,181	$24,732,083	$29,941,530	$5,209,447
Indiana	$4,276,401	$7,644,463	$6,883,187	-$761,276
Iowa	$2,193,017	$2,907,230	$2,369,957	-$537,273

Table 1. (Continued).

State or other area	2004 Actual	2005 Estimate	2006 Estimate	Change from 2005 estimate
Kansas	$2,975,681	$2,417,540	$3,001,512	$583,972
Kentucky	$1,812,413	$2,404,457	$2,427,174	$22,717
Louisiana	$2,328,221	$3,317,197	$1,322,119	-$1,995,078
Maine	$500,000	$500,000	$500,000	—
Maryland	$5,867,566	$6,654,183	$8,254,527	$1,600,344
Massachusetts	$9,673,186	$11,258,663	$12,943,819	$1,685,156
Michigan	$8,220,261	$11,540,302	$10,047,647	-$1,492,655
Minnesota	$6,108,755	$6,595,273	$7,232,358	$637,085
Mississippi	$971,870	$1,017,471	$753,405	-$264,066
Missouri	$3,130,233	$4,538,410	$5,088,266	$549,856
Montana	$500,000	$500,000	$500,000	—
Nebraska	$1,863,656	$2,143,231	$2,539,003	$395,772
Nevada	$5,706,721	$6,865,410	$9,110,190	$2,244,780
New Hampshire	$532,764	$1,056,420	$795,084	-$261,336
New Jersey	$16,278,278	$20,186,729	$21,314,703	$1,127,974
New Mexico	$5,494,409	$5,347,129	$4,714,268	-$632,861
New York	$47,907,904	$53,923,317	$52,235,038	-$1,688,279
North Carolina	$8,883,786	$9,979,375	$11,484,558	$1,505,183
North Dakota	$500,000	$500,000	$500,000	—
Ohio	$6,438,717	$6,567,211	$8,744,892	$2,177,681
Oklahoma	$2,916,153	$4,869,319	$3,517,558	-$1,351,761
Oregon	$4,951,822	$5,300,358	$5,768,467	$468,109
Pennsylvania	$9,383,763	$8,982,966	$11,518,404	$2,535,438
Rhode Island	$1,768,126	$2,375,164	$2,306,473	-$68,691
South Carolina	$2,442,675	$2,588,131	$3,007,497	$419,366
South Dakota	$534,980	$515,986	$701,006	$185,020
Tennessee	$3,686,302	$4,546,936	$4,235,980	-$310,956
Texas	$74,350,392	$82,422,240	$89,353,183	$6,930,943
Utah	$3,396,597	$2,888,015	$4,318,842	$1,430,827
Vermont	$500,000	$500,000	$500,000	—
Virginia	$7,273,394	$9,222,809	$9,094,619	-$128,190
Washington	$9,607,031	$8,547,438	$11,728,407	$3,180,969
West Virginia	$500,000	$610,998	$500,000	-$110,998
Wisconsin	$4,914,400	$6,171,980	$6,621,285	$449,305
Wyoming	$500,000	$500,000	$500,000	—
American Samoa	$1,161,870	$1,152,575	$1,152,575	—
Guam	$1,199,517	$1,189,921	$1,189,921	—
Northern Mariana Islands	$912,447	$905,147	$905,147	—
Puerto Rico	$2,725,136	$2,895,823	$3,117,307	$221,484
Virgin Islands	$132,241	$131,183	$131,183	—
Freely Associated States	—	—	—	—
Indian set-aside	$5,000,000	$5,000,000	$5,000,000	—
Other (non-State allocations)	$127,781,638	$88,221,851	$43,924,724	-$44,297,127
Total	$681,215,000	$675,765,000	$675,765,000	—

Source: U.S. Department of Education, Budget Service, Oct. 25, 2005.

REFERENCES

[1] In this report these two groups of students will be referred to as LEP students.

[2] U.S. Census Bureau, 1990 and 2000 Census Summary Files.

[3] Ibid.

[4] U.S. Department of Education, Annual Surveys of the States' Limited English Proficient Students and Available Educational Programs and Services, 1990-1998.

[5] According to *Assessment and Accountability Systems: 50 State Profiles*, by the Consortium for Policy Research in Education, all but one state (Iowa) required assessments by 2001.

[6] ESEA, §3113(b)(3)(C)(x). The assessment of LEP students will be discussed in greater detail later in this report. For further information on overall NCLBA assessments see CRS Report RL31407, *Educational Testing: Implementation of ESEA Title I-A Requirements Under the No Child Left Behind Act*, by Wayne Riddle.

[7] For more information, see CRS Report RL31487, Education for the Disadvantaged: Overview of ESEA Title I-A Amendments Under the No Child Left Behind Act, by Wayne Riddle.

[8] Title VII provided funds to SEAs and other eligible entities for numerous distinct language instructional programs and services. Part A, the Bilingual Education Act (BEA), awarded competitive grants for bilingual instructional and support services, professional development and foreign language instruction. Part C, the Emergency Immigrant Education Program, awarded formula grants to LEAs that recently experienced a large influx of immigrant students. Part B, the Foreign Language Assistance Program, is continued in the current reauthorization under Title V, Part D, Subpart 9. For further details on Title VII programs, see CRS Report 98-501, *Bilingual Education: An Overview*; CRS Report RS20042, *The Federal Emergency Immigrant Education Program*; and CRS Report RL31401, *Provisions for Limited English Proficient Students in H.R. 1, as Passed by the House and Senate*, all by Patricia Osorio-O'Dea.

[9] For the purposes of this report, the term "state" includes the District of Columbia and the Commonwealth of Puerto Rico.

[10] Under the four instructional services grants of the BEA (Title VII, Part A, Subpart 1), not more than 25% of the funds could be used for local programs that were "special alternative instructional programs" (i.e., that did not use students' native language in instruction).

[11] LEAs may test LEP students in non-English languages for an additional two years (i.e., five years total) if, on an individual pupil basis, it is determined that such accommodations would a provide more accurate and reliable assessment (§1111(b)(3)(C)(x)).

[12] For more information, see CRS Report RL31487, Education for the Disadvantaged: Overview of ESEA Title I-A Amendments Under the No Child Left Behind Act, by Wayne Riddle.

[13] Ibid.

[14] The Office of English Language Acquisition at ED has released a policy statement on this topic, available at [http://www.ed.gov/about/offices/ list/oela/ decofparentrights. doc].

[15] Available at [http://www.ed.gov/programs/nfdp/NRG1.2.25.03.doc].

[16] Available at [http://www.ed.gov/news/pressreleases/2004/02/02192004.html].

[17] The text from this press conference is available at [http://www.ed.gov/news/ pressreleases/2004/02/02192004.html].

[18] For more information, see CRS Report RL31487, Education for the Disadvantaged: Overview of ESEA Title I-A Amendments Under the No Child Left Behind Act; and CRS Report RL31407, Educational Testing: Implementation of ESEA Title I-A Requirements Under the No Child Left Behind Act, both by Wayne Riddle.

[19] However, ED has not made clear whether states which do this would also be required to hold first-year LEP students out of calculation of the "starting point" which is based on data for the 2001-2002 school year (§1111(2)(E)).

In: No Child Left Behind: Issues and Developments
Editor: P. H. Berkhart, pp. 131-135
ISBN: 978-1-60456-210-1

Chapter 7

MILITARY RECRUITMENT PROVISIONS UNDER THE NO CHILD LEFT BEHIND ACT: A LEGAL ANALYSIS*

Jody Feder

ABSTRACT

Under the No Child Left Behind Act (NCLBA) of 2001, which amended the Elementary and Secondary Education Act (ESEA), high schools that receive federal funds must provide certain student contact information to military recruiters upon request and must allow recruiters to have the same access to students as employers and colleges. Because the 110th Congress is likely to consider reauthorization of the ESEA, legislators may contemplate changes to the military recruitment provisions, either as part of the reauthorization or as stand-alone legislation. Currently, one bill, H.R. 1346, has been introduced in the 110th Congress. This report describes the NCLBA military recruitment provisions and discusses the legal issues that they may raise.

When Congress enacted the No Child Left Behind Act (NCLBA) of 2001,[1] it added several new requirements regarding the ability of military recruiters to access student information and to approach students directly. These new provisions — which are different from similar Department of Defense (DOD) provisions that allow DOD to compile directory information on high school students for military recruitment purposes or that require colleges and universities that receive federal funds to allow military recruiters on campus[2] — have proven to be somewhat controversial. Proponents of the recruitment provisions argue that the new law allows recruiters to inform students about the military opportunities available to them and eases the task of recruiting volunteers to sustain the nation's military forces. On the other hand, opponents contend that the provisions raise concerns about student privacy and should be changed to make it easier to opt out.[3] Currently, 95% of the country's school districts are estimated to be complying with the new requirements,[4] although it is important to note that, traditionally, most schools had already allowed military recruiters to contact students long before the NCLBA provisions became mandatory.[5]

The new NCLBA military recruitment provisions require high schools that receive federal funds to meet two requirements. First, such schools must "provide, on a request made by military recruiters ..., access to secondary school students names, addresses, and

---

* Excerpted from CRS Report RS22362, dated June 1, 2007.

telephone listings,"[6] and second, schools must "provide military recruiters the same access to secondary school students as is provided generally to post secondary educational institutions or to prospective employers of those students."[7] Schools that fail to comply with either of these two requirements — access to student information or equal access to students themselves — risk losing federal funds. However, private secondary schools that maintain a religious objection to military service are exempt from the recruitment provisions.[8]

Access to Student Information

As noted above, schools must, when requested, provide military recruiters with information concerning student names, addresses, and telephone numbers. Unlike more personal information such as Social Security numbers, this type of data is not protected by the Family Educational Rights and Privacy Act (FERPA),[9] which currently allows the release of student directory information in the absence of parental objections.[10] Thus, even before the NCLBA provisions were enacted, such student contact information was potentially available to outside entities.

Like FERPA, the NCLBA also provides the opportunity to opt out of the provisions requiring the release of directory information to military recruiters. Under the NCLBA, students or their parents may request that the student's directory information not be released without prior written consent. In addition, the local educational agency or private school must notify parents of their right to make such a request.[11]

Schools appear to have interpreted these opt out provisions in a variety of ways. For example, some schools have, as part of their compliance with an array of privacy laws, issued a general notice informing parents that they can opt out of the release of student contact information, while other schools have issued a separate and more explicit notice informing parents that such information may be released to the military for recruitment purposes if the parents do not opt out. Both of these types of notice appear to meet the statutory requirement regarding informing parents of their right to opt out, but recipients of the latter type of notice may be more likely to exercise that option. As a result, the type of notice that a school elects to provide has been a subject of debate.[12]

In addition, the notification provision has become controversial in part because schools have interpreted parental responses in different ways. For example, if parents fail to respond to the notice informing them of their right to opt out of the release of student information, some schools interpret the lack of response as indicating that the parent does not wish to opt out, while other schools interpret a lack of response as signifying that the parent does want to opt out. As a result, some interest groups have pressed legislators to clarify the law with regard to this point.[13]

Equal Access to Students

In addition to requiring schools to provide access to student information, the NCLBA also requires schools to provide access to students themselves. Specifically, schools must provide military recruiters the same access to students as is otherwise provided to other recruiters, such as private employers or institutions of higher education.[14] As with the notification provisions, schools have implemented the equal access provisions in a variety of ways. For example, some schools allow extensive access, permitting recruiters to set up information tables, visit classrooms, and freely approach students anywhere on campus. Other schools permit a lesser degree of access, and some restrict military access even further by forbidding information tables, requiring appointments before recruiters can meet students, and otherwise limiting access to campus.[15] Despite these variations in school policy, schools are allowed to place as many or as few restrictions as they wish on military recruiters, as long as schools treat such recruiters the same way they treat other entities that wish to contact students.

LEGAL CONCERNS

As noted previously, some opponents of the NCLBA military recruitment provisions have raised legal concerns about the new requirements. In particular, some critics have questioned whether the recruitment provisions violate a student's right to privacy, but neither statutory nor constitutional analysis appears to support this argument. Indeed, from a statutory perspective, the NCLBA provisions regarding release of student contact information are, as noted above, entirely consistent with FERPA, the longstanding law that protects the educational privacy rights of students. Likewise, the NCLBA military recruitment provisions, for the reasons discussed below, do not appear to raise constitutional concerns.

Under the auspices of the Fourteenth Amendment,[16] the Supreme Court has recognized that there is a constitutional right to privacy that protects against certain governmental disclosures of personal information,[17] but it has not established the standard for measuring such a violation. In the absence of explicit standards, the circuit courts have tended to establish a series of balancing tests that weigh the competing privacy interests and government interests in order to determine when information privacy violations occur.[18]

In *Falvo ex rel. Pletan v. Owasso Independent School District No. I-011*,[19] the Court of Appeals for the Tenth Circuit weighed the plaintiff's claim that peer grading and the practice of calling out grades in class resulted in an impermissible release of her child's education records in violation of FERPA. The plaintiff also claimed that the practice of peer grading violated her child's constitutional right to privacy. Although the court, in a holding that was later reversed by the Supreme Court,[20] ruled that the practice of peer grading violated FERPA, the Tenth Circuit denied the plaintiff's constitutional claim. In rejecting this claim, the court applied a three-part balancing test that considers "(1) if the party asserting the right has a legitimate expectation of privacy, (2) if disclosure serves a compelling state interest, and (3) if disclosure can be made in the least intrusive manner."[21] Based on the first prong of this test, the Tenth Circuit rejected the plaintiff's constitutional claim because it ruled that student's school work and test grades were not highly personal matters that deserved constitutional protection.[22]

Like peer graded student homework assignments, the release of student names, addresses, and telephone numbers to military recruiters would probably not be viewed by a court as violating a student's constitutional right to privacy under such a balancing test.

Unlike Social Security numbers or medical records, for example, it is unlikely that a court would hold that individuals have a legitimate expectation of privacy in the type of basic contact information that is typically found in a phone book. Furthermore, the government could argue persuasively that the release of such information serves a compelling state interest in facilitating the maintenance of the nation's armed forces. Finally, a court would probably view the disclosure required by the NCLBA as minimally intrusive, given that students can either opt out of the information release or decline to join the military, or both.

Ultimately, a court reviewing any privacy based challenge to the NCLBA military recruitment provisions would be likely to reject such a claim, especially in light of the fact that Congress was clearly acting within the scope of its constitutional authority when it enacted the military recruitment provisions of the NCLBA. Under the Spending Clause of the Constitution,[23] Congress frequently promotes its policy goals by conditioning the receipt of federal funds on state compliance with certain requirements. Indeed, the Supreme Court "has repeatedly upheld against constitutional challenge the use of this technique to induce governments and private parties to cooperate voluntarily with federal policy,"[24] and the Court recently reaffirmed this principle when, in response to a First Amendment challenge, it upheld similar military recruitment provisions that apply to colleges that receive federal funds.[25] Thus, the Court would likely uphold the NCLBA provisions in part on the basis of congressional authority under the Spending Clause.[26]

REFERENCES

[1] P.L. 107-110, 115 Stat. 1425.

[2] 10 U.S.C. §§ 503, 983. The requirements relating to institutions of higher education were recently the subject of a legal challenge, but the Supreme Court upheld the constitutionality of the statutory provisions requiring military access to college campuses that receive federal funds. Rumsfeld v. Forum for Academic and Institutional Rights, Inc., 126 S. Ct. 1297 (U.S. 2006). For more information, see CRS Report RS22405, *Military Recruiting and the Solomon Amendment: The Supreme Court Ruling in Rumsfeld v. FAIR*, by Charles V. Dale. For historical background on DOD provisions regarding military recruitment on high school and college campuses, see CRS Report RL30113, *Homosexuals and U.S. Military Policy: Current Issues*, by David F. Burrelli and Jody Feder. DOD recently published proposed regulations regarding military recruitment at institutions of higher education. Military Recruiting and Reserve Officer Training Corps Program Access to Institutions of Higher Education, 72 FR 25713 (proposed May 7, 2007).

[3] Tamar Lewin, "Uncle Sam Wants Student Lists, and Schools Fret," *N.Y. Times*, January 29, 2003, at B1.

[4] Alfred J. Sciarrino, From High School to Combat? No Child Left Behind!, 36 U. West. L.A. L. Rev. 94, 94 (2005).

[5] Lori Aratani, "Military Faces Parental Counterattack; High School Recruitment, a Longtime Tradition, Raises Worries in Wartime," *Wash. Post*, November 1, 2005, at B1.

[6] 20 U.S.C. § 7908(a)(1).

[7] *Id.* at § 7908(a)(3).
[8] *Id.* at § 7908(c).
[9] *Id.* at § 1232g. For more information on FERPA, see CRS Report RS22341, *The Family Educational Rights and Privacy Act: A Legal Overview*, by Jody Feder.
[10] 20 U.S.C. § 1232g(b)(1).
[11] *Id.* at 7908(a)(2).
[12] Aratani, *supra* note 5, at B1.
[13] *Id.*; *see also*, Michael Dobbs, "Schools and Military Face Off; Privacy Rights Clash With Required Release of Student Information," *Wash. Post*, June 19, 2005, at A3.
[14] 20 U.S.C. § 7908(a)(3).
[15] Dobbs, *supra* note 13, at A3.
[16] U.S. Const. amend. XIV, § 1.
[17] Whalen v. Roe, 429 U.S. 589 (1977).
[18] *See, e.g.*, Flanagan v. Munger, 890 F.2d 1557, 1570 (10th Cir. 1989); Plante v. Gonzalez, 575 F.2d 1119, 1134 (5th Cir. 1978).
[19] 233 F.3d 1203 (10th Cir. 2000).
[20] Owasso Indep. Sch. Dist. v. Falvo, 534 U.S. 426 (2002).
[21] Falvo ex rel. Pletan v. Owasso Indep. Sch. Dist. No. I-011, 233 F.3d 1203, 1208 (10th Cir. 2000).
[22] *Id.* at 1209.
[23] U.S. Const. art. I, § 8, cl. 1.
[24] Fullilove v. Klutznick, 448 U.S. 448, 474 (1980).
[25] Rumsfeld v. Forum for Academic and Institutional Rights, Inc., 126 S. Ct. 1297, 1306-07 (U.S. 2006).
[26] A search of the legal database Lexis-Nexis for cases involving challenges to the NCLBA military recruitment provisions revealed no results.

In: No Child Left Behind: Issues and Developments
Editor: P. H. Berkhart, pp. 137-142
ISBN: 978-1-60456-210-1

Chapter 8

PARAPROFESSIONAL QUALITY AND THE NO CHILD LEFT BEHIND ACT OF 2001*

Jeffrey J. Kuenzi

ABSTRACT

The No Child Left Behind Act of 2001 (NCLBA) established minimum qualifications for paraprofessionals employed in Title I, Part A-funded schools. Paraprofessionals in such schools who perform instructional duties were required to meet these qualifications by the end of the 2005-2006 school year. This report describes the act's paraprofessional quality requirements and discusses their implementation and specification through guidance by the U.S. Department of Education. The report concludes with some issues that may arise as the 110th Congress considers reauthorization of the Elementary and Secondary Education Act of 1965 (ESEA).

The No Child Left Behind Act of 2001 (NCLBA), signed into law on January 8, 2002 (P.L. 107-110), required that all paraprofessionals assigned instructional duties and employed in Title I, Part A-funded schools meet minimum qualifications by January 8, 2006.[1] The NCLBA states that paraprofessionals (also known as teacher aides) must have either completed two years of college, obtained an associate's degree, or demonstrated content knowledge and an ability to assist in classroom instruction. On June 17, 2005, the U.S. Department of Education (ED) announced that the paraprofessional deadline would be extended to the end of the 2005-2006 school year to coincide with the related NCLBA deadline for *highly qualified teachers*.[2]

The use of teacher aides in U.S. classrooms has been increasing every year since data on paraprofessionals were first collected by ED's National Center for Education Statistics. In 1980, teacher aides accounted for 11% of total full-time equivalent instructional staff; by 2001, they composed 17% of all instructional staff.[3] Paraprofessionals are also increasingly handling classroom responsibilities without supervision. An ED report issued in April 2000

* Excerpted from CRS Report RS22545, dated August 8, 2007.

indicated that 95% of paraprofessionals spent at least 60% of their time "teaching without a teacher present."[4] The report further revealed that paraprofessionals accounted for more than half of all Title I instructional staff — about 69,000 of all 135,000 full-time equivalent instructional personnel paid with Title I-A funds nationwide in the 1997-98 school year.

Recognition that the quality of instruction in U.S. schools is increasingly affected by the quality of paraprofessional staff has bolstered support for federal teacher aide standards. Prior to the NCLBA, the Elementary and Secondary Education Act of 1965 (ESEA) required only that paraprofessionals possess a high school diploma. This requirement was established in previous ESEA amendments passed under the Improving America's Schools Act of 1994 (P.L. 103-382).[5] Legislative proposals establishing higher standards for paraprofessionals were supported by ED under both the Clinton and Bush administrations, and were eventually enacted under the NCLBA.

As of the enactment of the NCLBA on January 8, 2002, all newly hired Title I paraprofessionals whose duties include instructional support must possess the minimum qualifications prior to employment. That is, they must have

- completed two years of study at an institution of higher education,
- obtained an associate's (or higher) degree, or
- passed a formal state or local academic assessment, demonstrating knowledge of and the ability to assist in instructing reading, writing, and mathematics.

Paraprofessionals hired on or before January 8, 2002, who were performing instructional duties in a program supported with Title I funds, were required to meet these requirements by the end of the 2005-06 school year.

The NCLBA paraprofessional qualification requirements apply *only* to Title I paraprofessionals with instructional duties; that is, those who

- provide one-on-one tutoring if the tutoring is scheduled at a time when a student would not otherwise receive instruction from a teacher;
- assist with classroom management, such as organizing instructional and other materials;
- provide assistance in a computer laboratory;
- conduct parental involvement activities;
- provide support in a library or media center;
- act as a translator; or
- provide instructional services to students under the direct supervision of a teacher.

Individuals who work in food services, cafeteria or playground supervision, personal care services, non-instructional computer assistance, and similar positions are not considered paraprofessionals, and do not have to meet these requirements. Also, ESEA Section 1119(e) indicates that paraprofessionals who *only* serve as translators or who *only* conduct parental involvement activities must have a secondary school diploma or its equivalent, but do not have to meet additional requirements.

The most recent non-regulatory guidance on paraprofessionals, issued by ED on March 1, 2004, clarifies a number of questions that have been raised during implementation of the NCLBA. The guidance describes various school settings under which paraprofessionals may or may not be required to meet the NCLBA rules. The requirements apply to *all* paraprofessionals employed in a schoolwide Title I program without regard to whether the position is funded with federal, state, or local funds. In targeted assistance Title I programs, only those paraprofessionals paid with Title I funds must meet the requirements (not those paid with state or local funds); however, special education paraprofessionals in targeted assistance programs must meet the requirements even if only part of their pay comes from Title I funds. A paraprofessional who provides services to private school students and is employed by a local education agency (LEA) with Title I funds must meet the NCLBA requirements; however, these requirements do not apply to those in the Americorps program, volunteers, or those working in either 21st Century Community Learning Centers or Head Start programs.

LEAs have discretion when it comes to considering who is an "existing" paraprofessional and whether *qualified* status is "portable." If an LEA laid off a paraprofessional who was initially hired on or before January 8, 2002, the LEA may consider that person an "existing" employee when the individual is subsequently recalled to duty. Also, an LEA may determine that a paraprofessional meets the qualification requirements if the individual was previously determined to meet these requirements by another LEA.

The ED guidance clarifies that "two years of study" means the equivalent of two years of full-time study as determined by an "institution of higher education" (IHE) — the definition of an IHE is specified in Section 101(a) of the Higher Education Act of 1965. Continuing education credits may count toward the two-year requirement if they are part of an overall training and development program plan and an IHE accepts or translates them to course credits.

Section C of the guidance discusses issues related to the assessment of paraprofessionals. The guidance indicates that a state or LEA may develop a paraprofessional knowledge and ability assessment using either a paper and pencil form, a performance evaluation, or some combination of the two. These assessments should gauge content knowledge (e.g., in reading, writing, and math) as well as competence in instruction (which may be assessed through observations). The content knowledge should reflect state academic standards and the skills expected of a child at a given school level.

The results of the assessment should establish a candidate's content knowledge and competence in instruction, and target the areas where additional training may be needed.

Most states are employing more than one type of written assessment along with performance evaluation. Two of the most common tests are ParaPro (developed by the Educational Testing Service) and WorkKeys (developed by the American College Testing Program). According to the Education Commission of the States (ECS), 36 states allow LEAs to use ParaPro for paraprofessional assessment, and 17 states allow the use of WorkKeys.[6] In addition, 21states allow LEAs to develop their own assessments. ECS considers 12 states to have established paraprofessional qualifications that exceed federal standards, and identifies 10 states that require paraprofessionals to obtain professional certification.[7] The ECS also identifies 11 states that have professional development programs for paraprofessionals.

Section D of the guidance discusses programmatic requirements that pertain to the supervision of paraprofessionals. The guidance points out that ESEA Section 1119(g)(3)(A) stipulates that paraprofessionals who provide instructional support must work under the "direct supervision" of a *highly qualified teacher*. Further, the guidance states the following:

> A paraprofessional works under the direct supervision of a teacher if (1) the teacher prepares the lessons and plans the instruction support activities the paraprofessional carries out, and evaluates the achievement of the students with whom the paraprofessional is working, and (2) the paraprofessional works in close and frequent proximity with the teacher. *[§200.59(c)(2) of the Title I regulations]* As a result, a program staffed entirely by paraprofessionals is not permitted.

In addition, the guidance states that the rules regarding direct supervision also apply to paraprofessionals who provide services under contract. That is, paraprofessionals hired by a third-party contractor to work in a Title I program must work under the direct supervision of a teacher (even though teachers employed by the contractor need not meet NCLBA *highly qualified teacher* requirements).

The ED guidance discusses funding sources for the professional development and assessment of paraprofessionals. An LEA must use not less than 5% of its Title I, Part A allocation for the professional development of teachers and paraprofessionals. LEAs may also use their general Title I funds for this purpose. Funds for professional development of paraprofessionals may also be drawn from Title II, Part A (for core subject-matter personnel); from Title III, Part A (for those serving English language learners); from Title V, Part A (for "Innovative" programs); and from Title VII, Part A, subpart 7 (for those serving Indian children). Schools and LEAs identified as needing improvement must reserve additional funds for professional development.

Section B-2 of the guidance describes conditions under which LEAs are prohibited from using Title I funds to hire new paraprofessionals. Such a prohibition may be imposed by a state on an LEA that has failed to make progress toward meeting the *annual measurable objectives* established by the state for increasing the percentage of *highly qualified teachers*, and has failed to make *adequate yearly progress* for three cumulative years.[8] Two exceptions to this rule are (1) if the hiring is to fill a vacancy created by the departure of another paraprofessional, and (2) if the hiring is necessitated by a significant increase in student enrollment or an increased need for translators or parental involvement personnel.

Forty-two states and the District of Columbia reported data to ED on the qualifications of their paraprofessionals for the 2003-2004 school year. Among them, 10 states reported that fewer than half of their paraprofessionals met the NCLBA requirements; four states reported that at least nine of every 10 of their paraprofessionals met these standards.[9] However, ED officials have recently indicated that most paraprofessionals acquired the minimum qualifications by the June 30, 2006, deadline.[10]

The NCLBA authorized Title I-A through FY2007. Although a one-year automatic extension through FY2008 is provided under the General Education Provisions Act, the NCLBA may be considered for reauthorization by the 110th Congress. Possible reauthorization issues concerning the paraprofessional provisions in Title I include the following:

- Are the assessments used to evaluate paraprofessional quality rigorous enough, and are they adequately tied to academic standards for students? Some consider the ParaPro and WorkKeys tests to be the "easy route," and claim they do not measure a teacher aide's ability to improve classroom instruction. Might a reauthorized ESEA be more explicit about the nature of these tests by linking them to other accountability provisions? Should ED be given greater authority to enforce higher standards for paraprofessional assessments?

- Should the paraprofessional qualification requirements be applied to a broader group of teacher aides? For example, should these requirements be applied to all paraprofessionals with instructional responsibilities, not just to those paid with Title I-A funds? Should the exceptions currently made for computer lab assistants, translators, and those assisting with parental involvement be curtailed? Is the language regarding "direct supervision" too vague or too difficult to enforce?
- Do current provisions for the professional development of teacher aides adequately encourage states to improve the paraprofessional workforce? Should states be given incentives to adopt paraprofessional certification requirements, as have been adopted in some states? Are there other ways to encourage paraprofessional development beyond the minimum qualifications that would positively affect the overall level of instructional quality?
- Have the paraprofessional qualification requirements significantly affected the extent to which Title I-A funds are used to hire these staff? In particular, have a significant number of paraprofessionals lost their jobs, or been assigned to non-Title I-A positions, after the end of the 2005-2006 school year because they were unable to meet the paraprofessional qualification requirements? Has this resulted in an overall decline or improvement in the quality of instruction?
- Should the roles of states versus LEAs in setting policies and implementing these requirements be clarified? Particularly in comparison to the teacher quality requirements of the NCLBA, there has been relatively little guidance from ED, or clarity in the statute, on state-versus-LEA roles in the area of paraprofessional qualification requirements. Has the result been a constructive form of flexibility or dysfunctional ambiguity?

REFERENCES

[1] Section 1119(c) states that all paraprofessionals newly hired after the date of enactment be *highly qualified*, and section 1119(d) states that those hired prior to enactment be *highly qualified* not later than four years after enactment.

[2] This announcement is at [http://www.ed.gov/news/pressreleases/2005/06/06172005a.html]. For more information on the *highly qualified teacher* requirement, see CRS Report RL33333, *A Highly Qualified Teacher in Every Classroom: Implementation of the No Child Left Behind Act*, by Jeffrey J. Kuenzi.

[3] U.S. Education Department, *Digest of Education Statistics, 2005*, table 78, available at [http://nces.ed.gov/programs/digest/d05/tables/dt05_078.asp].

[4] U.S. Education Department, *Study of Educational Resources and Federal Funding*, Washington, DC, April 2000.

[5] Prior to those amendments, the ESEA was silent on this issue dealing with paraprofessionals.

[6] ECS Issue Brief, Instructional Paraprofessional Statistics and Trends, Denver, CO, September 2005.

[7] Ibid. Paraprofessional qualification requirements for each state can be found on ECS's online interactive paraprofessional database, which is available at [http://www.ecs.org/ecsmain.asp?page=/html/educationIssues/teachingQuality/parapro/NCLB_parapro_DB_intro.asp].

[8] For more information on the *highly qualified teacher* requirement, see CRS Report RL33333, *A Highly Qualified Teacher in Every Classroom: Implementation of the No Child Left Behind Act*, by Jeffrey J. Kuenzi. For more information on the adequate yearly progress, see CRS Report RL32495, *Adequate Yearly Progress (AYP): Implementation of the No Child Left Behind Act*, by Wayne C. Riddle.

[9] These reports were obtained from ED by *Education Week* through a Freedom of Information Act (FOIA) request and published on March 16, 2005; a state-by-state table is available at [http://www.edweek.org/media/27admin.pdf].

[10] According to an *Education Week* article published on August 30, 2006; available at [http://www.edweek.org/ew/articles/2006/08/30/01paras.h26.html?qs=paraprofessional].

INDEX

D

E

F

G

M

N

O

P

Q

R

S

T